About the Author

JACQUELINE SHANNON is a San Diego–based journalist and author who has written both for children and about children, for teens and about teens. She has published eight young adult novels and has written frequently for *Seventeen*, *Teen*, *YM*, and *Cosmopolitan*. She is the author of *The New Mother's Body Book*, *Dream Doll*, and *Raising a Star*.

MADELINE TROBAUGH, Jacqueline Shannon's daughter, attends Mills College in the San Francisco Bay Area.

WHY IT'S GREAT TO BE A GIRL

Also by Jacqueline Shannon

NONFICTION

Raising a Star: The Parent's Guide to Helping Kids Break into Theater,
Film, Television, or Music
Cowritten with Nancy Carson

The Wedding Dress Diet: Lose Weight and Look Great on Your Wedding
Day and Beyond
Cowritten with Robyn Flipse, R.D.

Dream Doll: The Ruth Handler Story
Cowritten with Ruth Handler

The New Mother's Body Book: How Having a Baby Will Change Your
Body, Your Mind, and Your Marriage Forever

FICTION FOR YOUNG ADULTS

It's in Your Hands, Daisy P. Duckwitz

I Hate My Hero

Why Would Anyone Have a Crush on Horace Beemis?

Faking It

Big Guy, Little Women

Upstaged

Too Much T.J.

WHY IT'S GREAT TO BE A GIRL

50 Awesome Reasons Why We Rule!

Jacqueline Shannon

with her daughter, Madeline Trobaugh

HARPER

NEW YORK · LONDON · TORONTO · SYDNEY

HARPER

A paperback version of this book was published in 1994 by Warner Books.

WHY IT'S GREAT TO BE A GIRL. Copyright © 1994, 2007 by Jacqueline Shannon. All rights reserved. Printed in the United States of America. No part of this book may be used or reproduced in any manner whatsoever without written permission except in the case of brief quotations embodied in critical articles and reviews. For information address HarperCollins Publishers, 10 East 53rd Street, New York, NY 10022.

HarperCollins books may be purchased for educational, business, or sales promotional use. For information please write: Special Markets Department, HarperCollins Publishers, 10 East 53rd Street, New York, NY 10022.

First Harper paperback published 2007.

Designed by Nancy Singer Olaguera, ISPN Publishing Services

Library of Congress Cataloging-in-Publication Data has been applied for.

ISBN: 978-0-06-117214-4 (pbk.)
ISBN-10: 0-06-117214-6 (pbk.)

07 08 09 10 11   ISPN/RRD   10 9 8 7 6 5 4 3 2 1

For Madeline—

As a precocious preschooler, you inspired the first
Why It's Great to Be a Girl. *As you grew into the young*
woman you are today, you've made me so proud
that someday I may be writing a book called
Why It's Great to Have Had THIS Girl.
Thanks for your help.

Many Thanks

. . . to Linda Konner, as usual, Queen of the Literary Agents. That should be her ™.

. . . to HarperCollins' Sarah Durand, one of the nicest editors I've ever worked with, and Jeremy Cesarec, for their input and enthusiasm for this project.

. . . to my parents, Dr. E. J. Farmer and the late Louise Ann Farmer, who never once said "Girls can't/shouldn't do that." Dad: Sorry about #4, but we have to go with the facts! Mom: Every night I see you shining like a diamond in the sky.

. . . to Emma Biegacki of *Mad Hot Ballroom*. I have never met her or spoken to her, but she inspired and convinced me to update and expand the original version of this book.

. . . to Radia Perlman, the Mother of the Internet, who made doing the research for this book so much easier than the first time around. (See #41.)

. . . to Carleen Hemric and Phil Giannangeli, the two junior high school teachers who have followed and supported my career for all these years. At a time when my confidence was shaky, Carleen persuaded me that I had writing talent.

. . . to Dan Baits, of Helix Charter High School, who did the same thing for my daughter.

. . . to Linda Olander, with apologies that "Women Make Great Bosses" had to be cut for space reasons.

. . . to Reginald Calvin, my best friend and sparring partner. Write your own book!

Finally, I want to honor the late pioneering businesswoman Ruth Handler, whose autobiography I cowrote, and crusader Doris Tate, whose autobiography I was sadly never able to finish. These women, who are discussed in this book, taught me much about having a vision, finding one's niche, and taking the initiative.

—Jacqueline Shannon

Introduction

In the summer of 2005, my then sixteen-year-old daughter Madeline and I squealed with delight (and startled a few of our fellow theater-goers) when a girl in the sleeper-hit documentary *Mad Hot Ballroom* plugged my 1994 book *Why It's Great to Be a Girl*.

In the documentary, several groups of eleven-year-olds in mostly inner-city schools face the highs, the heartbreaks, and sometimes the humiliation of competitive ballroom dancing. In a few scenes, some of the girls are complaining about the atti-tudes, behaviors, and the "givens" of their male partners. "Why," bristled one, "do THEY always get to lead?" At one point, silence. Then Emma, who the film's Web site (www.paramountclassics .com/madhot) describes as a "typical New York kid [who] always has something meaningful to say" and who "stands out as the girl who is wise beyond her years," suddenly blurts out, "Look, I read this book called *Why It's Great to Be a Girl*, and I learned that . . ."

My daughter and I were so excited that we barely heard her exact words. I just knew that they were extremely positive. And we both came away with the opinion that the book, in at least some small way, contributed to Emma's confidence and her ability to speak up when it's important.

The first edition of *Why It's Great to Be a Girl* has been out of print for years, but, in retrospect, I shouldn't have been as surprised at Emma's comment as I was. Through the years, friends of friends, friends of cousins, and coworkers have found used copies of *Why It's Great to Be a Girl* to give as gifts and have asked me to autograph them, although I warned them, "A lot of the facts in that book are very outdated."

Our world has changed dramatically since 1992–1993, when I was researching and writing the book. Madeline was four. She graduated from high school with a 4.3 GPA, she plays a mean clarinet (she was in both marching band and wind symphony), and she was frequently called upon during her high school years to boost morale, not just in the band but also among non-band students. As her "senior project," she started a business designing and manufacturing T-shirts that don't bash males but that empower teen girls. Madeline won the 2005–2006 Helix High School English Department Outstanding Student of the Year honor. She was awarded a substantial merit scholarship to one of California's best private colleges, where she is now a freshman.

I am not saying that she's perfect. One example: her room has always been a pigsty. And I don't mean to imply that her successes and self-confidence are solely due to my book or the parenting she received. She has had several excellent role models over the years, many of them teachers (both women *and* men), who have boosted her confidence in her abilities. She is also an insatiable reader of certain genres of fiction from which she has derived strong convictions of her own.

This book is a longer (women have achieved a lot since the early 1990s!) and very revised and updated version of the original. That book was one of the first books written about self-esteem for girls. I got the idea for the book because my own daughter, a preschooler, was encountering sexism even at that early age. Here is just one of the examples that I listed in the introduction to the original version of the book:

> An elderly man walking his dog through a park stops to talk to a little girl [that would be Madeline] who is climbing the monkey bars. "When I grow up, I'm going to be a ballerina and a doctor," she tells the man.
>
> "You let the boys be the doctors," the man replies. "Girls don't have the stomach to deal with blood."

Tee-hee. Madeline is now working toward a bachelor of science degree in nursing and plans to go on to get a master's degree in midwifery. I wanted to counteract those doses of boy bias by building up Madeline's pride in her own gender while not bashing guys.

The other thing that spurred me on at the time were the results of some very discouraging studies. For example, a 1991 American Association of University Women (AAUW) study found that only 29 percent of young teenage girls were "happy the way I am," compared to the 60 percent who gave that response back in elementary school and in marked contrast to their teenage boy counterparts, whose self-images had been judged much more positive.

Carol Gilligan, who was then head of Harvard's Project on the Psychology of Women and the Development of Girls, had found that one of the ways teenage girls exhibit their wavering confidence is by becoming more tentative in offering opinions—a trait that she said often persists into adulthood. A Gilligan example at the time: When she interviewed one girl at age twelve, the girl answered "I don't know" only 21 times; at the age of fourteen, the same girl's "I don't know" number shot up to 135.

I realized that those studies mirrored my own experience twenty-something years earlier. I had been something of a childhood star—the whiz kid who skipped grades in elementary school, edited the school paper, was always voted the class president or team captain. But something happened to me along about the time I turned fourteen. Although I can't remember any specific incidents that triggered it (it was probably largely due to my rapidly changing body), I completely lost my self-confidence and basically skulked my way through high school and then college too. I did not really get my old self-confidence back till I was past thirty. The original *Why It's Great to Be a Girl* was my part in helping to ensure that that didn't happen to later generations of girls.

I would say overall that in the years since the original version was published, self-esteem among white and African American girls has improved (recent studies, in fact, have shown that African American girls have higher self-esteem than any other race). But it's still not as high as it should be, especially among minorities other than African Americans. Over the years, Madeline attended well-integrated public schools in Southern California and made friends with a variety of girls who weren't white. When they all became teens, my daughter, dismayed, began to tell me that many of her friends were encountering bias from their families because their cultures historically value males more than females.

It is not my intention to interfere with or try to change other cultures. I simply feel that girls like these will get a boost from *Why It's Great to Be a Girl*. I also hope to reach an international audience of girls who live in countries in which gender bias is even more prevalent than in the Western countries. For these reasons, this new version is more multicultural (to reflect the increasing multiculturalism in Western countries) and global (the original version pretty much focused on women's accomplishments in the Western countries, especially the United States). It is also the reason that, while the original book was primarily intended for mothers of young daughters and, to a much-less-stressed extent, to girls entering adolescence, this edition was written for YOU as well—a girl or young woman who can read on her own.

So check out how much you've got going for yourself. I promise you, by the time you finish this book, you'll be in awe of what your gender has achieved, full of pride about the special talents and strengths of your female body and mind, and fully convinced, once and forever, that it really is great to be a girl.

—*Jacqueline Shannon*
San Diego, California

WHY IT'S GREAT TO BE A GIRL

The most frequently sung song of all time was written by women.

Mildred Hill and Patty Smith Hill wrote the music that was to become "Happy Birthday to You" in 1893. It became the first song ever sung in space (at least by earthlings!) on March 8, 1969, when the astronauts aboard *Apollo 9* sang it for Christopher Kraft, director of space operations for NASA. Contrary to popular belief, "Happy Birthday" is not in the public domain. Hill set up a foundation to which a royalty is supposed to be paid for each entertainment use of the song—when it's sung on a sitcom, for example. Or at your birthday party!

Actually, it's the most frequently sung song in the English language, according to the *Guinness Book of World Records*. It's been translated into many other languages, but, oddly, it is often sung with the English lyrics in countries where English is not a primary language.

Incidentally, a woman, Euphemia Allen, also composed what is probably the song played most often on the piano—"Chopsticks"!

Speaking of musical achievement . . .

We sing better than guys do.

Six times as many females as males can sing in tune. Why? No expert claims to have the definitive answer. But most speculate that better singing is a part of the female's superior verbal-ability package (see #5). Others point to the fact that females have superior auditory memory (see #25)—that is, we are better at remembering the way a song is supposed to sound, say, from hearing it on the radio. It probably also doesn't hurt that mothers tend to sing more to girl babies than to boy babies, according to some studies.

Women invented many of the devices that make our everyday lives easier.

· ·

In 1957 C. D. Tuska, the patent director for RCA, a company that makes TVs, audiovisual equipment, and the like, said: "Most of our inventors are of the male sex. Why is the percentage of women so low? I'm sure I do not know, except the Good Lord intended them to be mothers. They produce the inventors and help rear them, and that should be sufficient." Well, shut it, Tuska.

Women invented the dishwasher, for example, plus disposable diapers, the bra (and the jockstrap!), flat-bottomed paper bags, Scotchgard (to make things waterproof), vacuum canning, the automatic sewing machine, and the drip coffee maker. Women also invented Jell-O and the TV dinner (although the early TV dinners were terrible—take it from one who knows).

In 1793 the first-ever U.S. patent was issued to Hannah Slater for perfecting cotton sewing thread. In the early 1900s Madame C. J. Walker created the first cosmetics and hair care products specifically for African Americans. A little later in the century Dorothy Feiner Rodgers, the wife of famous composer Richard Rodgers (he cowrote the songs for *The Sound of Music*, for example) and a wealthy member of New York's high society, surprisingly invented a couple of rather basic household items. The more popular of the two was called the Jonny Mop, and it is still being manufactured today. A small mop to

clean toilets, it was the first that featured a disposable sponge on its
. . . uh . . . icky end.

But women inventors haven't limited themselves to hearth,
home, and hair. If you want to go way, way back in time, Greek schol-
ars believe Queen Semiramis of Assyria invented bridges, causeways,
and canals. The list of woman-borne inventions also includes the bul-
letproof vest, the fire escape, the Navy's signal flare, the circular saw,
solar heating, invisible glass, computer programming, DuPont's Kevlar
(a thread that's as strong as steel), Liquid Paper correction fluid (usually
referred to as "white-out"), pneumatic (inflated with air) tires, tract
housing, the cordless phone, laser cataract surgery, windshield wipers,
the hang glider, and even the white line that divides a road.

Amelia Earhart, who, in 1932, was the first woman to fly solo
across the Atlantic, designed the first lightweight luggage designed for
air travel. Hedy Lamarr (a famous 1930s film star) invented a sophisti-
cated and hush-hush torpedo control device to foil the Nazis, a device
that now speeds satellite communications throughout the world. Ruth
Handler, best known as the inventor of the Barbie doll, also invented
the first truly natural-looking breast prosthesis for women who had
had mastectomies. Elsa Garmire, now a professor of engineering at
Dartmouth College, developed a cost-effective method of zapping
graffiti with a laser (this is one of nine patents she owns). Incidentally,
she started the first commercial laser light show, "Laserium," while she
lived in California.

Experts believe women invented scores of other useful contrap-
tions we now take for granted, but they never received any credit for

their work. Many American women, especially those who did their inventing before 1900, registered patents under their husband's or their father's name because (1) women had no property rights until the turn of the century, and (2) to be mechanical was considered unfeminine.

A case in point: Have you ever heard of Catherine Littlefield Greene? She was evidently behind the invention of a machine that changed the course of American history. In 1792 Greene, a widow with five children, was running a boardinghouse in Georgia. When she became annoyed with the amount of time she had to spend separating cotton from its seeds so that she could spin it into thread, she prodded a young boarder named Eli Whitney to come up with a machine to do the work for her. With Greene's financial support, Whitney enthusiastically tackled the problem and, after about six months, came up with a prototype of the cotton gin, then almost gave up because the wooden teeth he had devised to separate the seeds from the cotton just weren't tough enough for the job. It was Greene who suggested he try wire teeth instead. The rest is history. And that's a conservative version of the story. Some accounts have Greene actually providing Whitney with the plans for the machine.

Wherever the truth lies, it's a fact that Greene didn't get in on the patent and that the machine had immense historical repercussions. It enabled the South to develop a thriving economy based on cotton, which required the revival of the dying slave trade so that there would be enough labor to pick the enormous amount of cotton soon needed to meet worldwide demand. And that increase in the importing and ownership of slaves would lead to America's Civil War.

On a lighter note, a woman is also credited with having invented the ice cream cone. We don't know her name, just that she was the female companion of one Charles E. Menches, who, while attending the 1904 Louisiana Purchase Exposition in St. Louis, bought her an ice cream sandwich and a bunch of flowers. The resourceful lady rolled up one wafer of the sandwich to serve as a holder for the flowers, then rolled up the other wafer for the ice cream. The cone was born.

BONUS! A woman came up with the idea for the job of flight attendant.

In 1930, two years before Amelia Earhart's record-setting solo flight, Ellen Church became the world's first flight attendant (then called a skygirl and later a stewardess). Church was both a pilot and a registered nurse. She applied to Boeing Air Transport for a pilot position but was turned down because of her gender. Commercial air travel had been slowly gaining in popularity in the 1920s, but many people were worried that it wasn't safe. So when Church wasn't allowed to pilot, she suggested placing nurses on board passenger planes to ease the public's fears. Boeing liked the idea and hired her, and other airlines followed suit, but nursing qualifications were soon loosened.

By the way, in the early years of commercial flight, flight attendants had to be female, were forced to retire when they turned thirty-two or got married, and couldn't be taller than five-foot-four or weigh more than 115. Ouch!

Overall, we drive better than men do.

In the United States alone, more than forty thousand people are killed on the road each year, and according to the Insurance Institute for Highway Safety, more of those people are men than women. According to several reports, men, especially young men (between the ages of sixteen and twenty-five) drive more aggressively than women. They tend to take out their aggression in a direct manner (say, tailgating to a dangerous extent) than in an indirect manner (say, just shaking a fist). What's more, men are more likely to break traffic laws and to take more risks while driving. In younger males this "daredevil" driving has been attributed to "factors such as emotional immaturity and misplaced feelings of immortality," according to an expert at the Insurance Information Institute.

Finally, according to one recent fascinating study, estrogen (the primary sex hormone in females) may contribute to our better driving. British researcher Amarylis Fox of the University of Bradford School of Pharmacy tested young to middle-aged adults on spatial memory, planning, attention, motor control, and rule learning. Women consistently outperformed men in learning rules and shifting their attention, helpful qualities for drivers.

"This study demonstrates that tasks requiring mental flexibility favor women over men, an area not previously considered to elicit strong sex differences," Fox says in a news release. "Driving could be a good example of how this is applied to everyday life." She added that estrogen may make a difference in those areas.

Girls are better with words.

Remember how the boys in preschool used to hit and push when they were angry, instead of "using their words"?

Girls begin to speak earlier than boys do and are better readers at school, speak more fluently, understand what is said better, and learn foreign languages more easily. This is true whether we live in Nepal, the Netherlands, or Nebraska. We retain this edge in communication ability throughout our lives. Here are some theories about why this is true:

First, certain areas connecting the right and left sides of the brains are larger and contain more connections in females than in males, leading researchers to conclude that females use both sides of the brain more frequently than males do. Female brains are simply better organized for communication between the two sides. And according to neuropsychiatrist Louann Brizendine, the brain areas for language are larger in women than in men. Brizendine, author of *The Female Brain* (2006), also says that the hippocampus part of the brain—the site of emotions and memory information—is also larger in women than in men. It is easier for us to express our emotions and to remember the details of emotional events (such as exactly what you and your boyfriend were wearing on the day you first met).

Finally, anthropologist Helen E. Fisher considers the most compelling argument for women's verbal superiority to be its link to the good female hormone estrogen. She once recounted a study of two hundred women of childbearing age and their verbal skills during their menstrual cycles. In one example, the women were asked to repeat a tongue twister like "A box of mixed biscuits in a biscuit mixture." In the middle of their menstrual cycles, when estrogen levels are at their highest, they could accomplish this much better than they could when their monthly periods had ended, because that's when estrogen levels are much lower.

We also talk more than guys do. In most countries, women have a "verbal output" of around 7,000 words a day, compared to a man's 3,000, according to Dennie Hughes, an award-winning journalist and columnist for *USA Weekend* magazine, among other publications.

Incidentally, scientists have acknowledged the superiority of women's language skills for generations. Here, for example, from Canadian psychologist D. O. Hebb's ancient (1958) *Textbook of Psychology*, is a snappy comeback to any guy who discounts the value of female verbal talent: "Males, who are inclined to think that verbal skill is due simply to talking too much, may be reminded that language is [hu]man's distinguishing mark as a species."

We hold on to our verbal skills longer than guys do.

According to a University of Pennsylvania study, men probably lose their verbal abilities faster than women. Using magnetic resonance imaging—a kind of X-ray without the radiation—researchers studied the brains of thirty-four men and thirty-five women. They found that deterioration in the brain— especially on the left side of the brain that controls language and verbal ability—was two to three times faster in men. How do the researchers account for that? They speculate that our female hormones "may protect the brain from atrophy [shrinking] associated with aging." Previous studies have shown that these hormones increase blood flow to the brain—that may be what's providing the protection.

Women are also superior at nonverbal communication.

That is, we are better at sensing the difference between what people say and what they mean. We're better at reading other people's emotional cues—for example, the facial wince, nervous hand clenching, and other subconscious signals that a person is feeling guilty. According to relationship expert Dennie Hughes, numerous studies have shown that 70 to 80 percent of communication is nonverbal.

Mother Nature probably bestowed this skill on us so that we can better mother infants who aren't yet able to communicate their needs verbally. Like language ability, the skill is attributed to the particular setup, patterns, and interactions of the female brain . . . making "women's intuition" a scientific reality.

And here's something pretty cool: Psychologist Joyce Brothers once wrote that she believes it's this skill that will eventually make females the dominant gender. She predicts that in the future, physical strength—which has kept males dominant until now—may become about as necessary as the appendix is today.

"The key to survival in the nuclear age is going to be perception, the ability to sense how others feel about an event or an issue or a threat and what they are likely to do about it," she wrote. "Everyone can think of episodes in our foreign policy that illustrate a serious lack of perception. As more women enter government and politics at the higher policy-making levels, I am convinced there will be fewer such episodes."

We make up our minds faster.

Researchers believe women can make faster decisions because we more frequently put *both* sides of our brains to work on a problem. Here's how one researcher expressed it: "Think of the brain as a city divided in half by a river. In the female brain, because there are so many bridges over the river, traffic moves faster and more efficiently between the two halves."

Here's a more scientific explanation. In 2005 Richard Haier of the University of California at Irvine announced the findings he and colleagues had come up with after a thorough study of the brain. The brain is mostly made up of stuff called gray matter and white matter. Gray matter represents the information processing centers. White matter works to network these processing centers. Men think more with their gray matter; women think more with the white. The researchers found that, in general, males have almost 6.5 times the amount of gray matter related to general intelligence than women do. But women have 10 times the amount of white matter related to intelligence as men.

"These findings suggest that human evolution has created two different types of brains designed for equally intelligent behavior," Haier told a reporter.

Anthropologists and archaeologists credit females with the "civilization" of humankind.

As Elizabeth Gould Davis stated in her book *The First Sex*, "Women dragged man, kicking and screaming, out of savagery into the New Stone Age." How? According to Buckminister Fuller, who was an American visionary, inventor, architect, and designer, "Women organized the home crew to pound the corn, comb the wool, dry the skins, etc. They invented pottery and weaving, discovered how to keep foods by cold storage or by cooking. Women, in fact, invented industrialization."

We're also credited with beginning the domestication of animals and—most important of all—with inventing agriculture. "While [man] enjoyed himself, [women] observed that the seeds dropped on the midden pile produced newer and bigger plants," wrote Kenneth MacGowan and Joseph A. Hester, Jr., in *Early Man in the New World*. Out of the invention of agriculture, the authors continued, "rose a settled community and a surplus of provender which allowed the few . . . to think and plan and build a civilization." MacGowan and Hester believe that women also invented milling stones to grind seeds, and they speculated that "as she watched the wearing away of mortar and pestle and milling stone as she ground her flour between them the idea occurred to her . . . that it was possible to grind stones into axes and other implements." If that was true, we can also pat ourselves on the back for inventing manufacture!

What motivated us to be so inventive? Davis believes it is because woman has eternally struggled "to make the best of things, to provide food and shelter for her children, to make 'home' comfortable for them, to soften and brighten their lives, and to make the world a safer and more pleasant place for them to grow in."

Women smell better than men.

We're talking BO here. The human sweat gland is called the apocrine gland—and there are hundreds of these in the human armpit, scientifically known as the axillary. "Sure there are some first-class women stinkers," Albert Kligman, M.D., a University of Pennsylvania dermatologist once said in *Health* magazine. But, added Kligman, the apocrine gland is androgen-driven. Androgens are male hormones, though women have some too. "Men have more androgen and bigger apocrine glands, and they stink more."

Compounding the problem is the fact that males aren't as aware as females of whether or not they smell because . . .

Women also smell better than men!

Women are more sensitive to odors than men are. A 1985 test of some two thousand noses at the Smell and Taste Center at the Hospital of the University of Pennsylvania is one of several studies that prove it. Another is the huge and now famous *National Geographic* magazine's 1986 "Smell Survey" of 1.5 million of its readers. The respondents had been sent six encapsulated odors: sweat, banana, musk, cloves, a natural gas warning agent, and a synthetic rose scent. An accompanying questionnaire asked them to identify the scents, rank them by their level of pleasantness, and so on.

Interestingly, the smelling ability of females actually gets even better once we're through puberty. Researchers tie this skill to female hormones . . . specifically, and once again, to estrogen. When estrogen levels are highest—at ovulation—a woman's olfactory sensitivity can increase up to a whopping one thousand times (not that this is always a good thing!). Because of the hormonal tie, it seems obvious Mother Nature felt superschnozzes were somehow needed for reproductive purposes. It's been proven to a statistically scientific degree that mothers of six-hour-old babies can find their own baby among a group of others by smell alone, whereas males cannot.

A corroborating anecdote: A residential repair worker at San Diego Gas and Electric tells customers to always trust a woman's nose.

"I've seen heated arguments between husband and wife—she says she smells a gas leak; he insists that he doesn't," the repairman says. "In all my years on the job, the woman has been right every single time."

BONUS! Girls' voices don't "crack" during puberty.

When a boy's voice begins to deepen during puberty, he has to go through an embarrassing stage when his voice can crack or even squeak without warning. Oftentimes, it happens at the worst possible moment, the moment of high stress, such as when he is asked a question in class. What's happening is that his vocal cords have begun to double in size, and he has to relearn how to control the pitch and sound they produce. Yes, female vocal cords increase in size, and our voices change during puberty too. But according to medical experts, the increase in size is only about 30 percent, and the change is much more smooth and gradual—nothing, as a writer for *Teen* magazine once put it, to "crack up" about.

Some of history's most effective and powerful leaders have been queens.

Poland's Queen Jadwiga (1370–1399), for example, is considered one of that country's greatest rulers as well as one of the truly inspired peacemakers of history, according to anthropologist Ashley Montagu. "England's Queen Elizabeth I and Victoria rank among the greatest of English monarchs," he added in his book *The Natural Superiority of Women*.

When Elizabeth I became queen in the sixteenth century, England was in a horrible state. The country had just lost a war against France, the royal treasury was depleted, and England's citizens, hostile and resentful after Mary Tudor's bloody and bigoted reign, were still fighting with one another over the question of England's religion: Was the country Catholic or Protestant? When Elizabeth died, England was the richest and most powerful country in the world. During the golden years of her reign—dubbed the Elizabethan Age in her honor—the country became the Mistress of the Seas by defeating the Spanish Armada and expanding its trading and holdings throughout the world. Elizabeth was also the monarch who made the Church of England the country's official religion.

The reign of Queen Victoria was also an era of extreme prosperity and prestige for England. In fact, some historians consider the late 1890s—when Victoria was celebrating sixty years on the throne—to be the time the country was at its peak of power. Supposedly, when Victoria died, England's citizens were so grief stricken that all of the stores sold out of black cloth.

Russia's Catherine the Great (1729–1796) reigned over the country's pre-Revolution expansion into one of the world's major powers. She added the Crimea, the Ukraine, Lithuania, and Poland to the Russian empire. Some of the many social reforms she instituted included establishing free hospitals and schools throughout the country, building new towns, highways, and canals, promoting religious tolerance, reforming the tax system, standardizing the laws and the currency so that they no longer differed among Russian provinces, and improving the living and working conditions of the serfs.

Queen Isabella was at the helm when Spain first reached the world leadership position it would hold in the 1400s and 1500s. She united the splintered country, and because of that and its growing number of colonies in the New World, Spain became for a time the most powerful country in Europe.

And during the sixteenth-century reign of Queen Catherine de Medici, writes Elizabeth Gould Davis in *The First Sex*, "France rose to her status as the cultural and intellectual center of the world—a status maintained down to our own time."

Marveling at the success of queens, one eighteenth-century male scholar speculated that the "lenity and moderation" of females make women "fitter for good administration than [the] severity and roughness" of you-know-who.

11

Two females initiated the discovery and colonization of the land that would become the United States of America.

Two of the aforementioned queens, as a matter of fact.

True, the Indians were in America first, but Europeans have always gotten the credit for "discovering" and colonizing the United States as we now know it. And the first of those—Christopher Columbus—was able to go for it only because Spain's Queen Isabella gave him the money he needed for his trip. While other higher-ups in Spain wrote off as impossible the idea that the confident but penniless Columbus could sail directly west to reach the Indies—instead of taking the usual route around the tip of Africa—Isabella believed so strongly in Columbus that she pledged her crown jewels to finance the expedition.

In 1578, fifty-four years after Isabella died, England's Queen Elizabeth I, who was far more interested in exploring the new land than her grandfather (Henry VII) or her father (Henry VIII) had been, issued the first patent for English colonization of the New World's mainland. In issuing this patent, Elizabeth stipulated that no Englishman would lose his citizenship rights by moving to the New World. It was this assurance that encouraged thousands of English citizens to head west over the next two hundred years, which ultimately resulted in the birth of the United States.

Women currently hold the highest office in several countries of the world.

12

Yep. While the United States still hasn't had a female president (although that *will* happen in your lifetime), other countries are more enlightened. Current women heads of state and government include:

* Michelle Bachelet, President of Chile (2006–)
* Helen Clark, Prime Minister of New Zealand (1999–)
* Luisa Diogo, Prime Minister of Mozambique (2004–)
* Tarja K. Halonen, President of Finland (2000–)
* Ellen Johnson-Sirleaf, President of Liberia (2006–)
* Chandrika Kumaratunga, President of Sri Lanka (1994–)
* Gloria Macapagal-Arroyo, President of the Philippines (2001–)
* Mary McAleese, President of Ireland (1997–)
* Angela Merkel, Chancellor of Germany (2005–)
* Yulia Timoshenko, Prime Minister of Ukraine (2005–)
* Varia Vike-Freiberga, President of Latvia (1999–)
* Khaleda Zia, Prime Minister of Bangladesh (1991–1996, 2001–)

Time for a cool anecdote: Margaret Thatcher was Great Britain's prime minister for an almost unprecedented three consecutive terms, from 1979 to 1990. According to the *Washington Post*, a whole generation of British kids was brought up so accustomed to the idea of a female leading their country that when Thatcher was replaced by John Major, a child asked, "But Daddy, can a *man* be prime minister?"

WHY IT'S GREAT TO BE A GIRL

Except for muscles, the female body is stronger than the male body in every way.

Women have greater stamina and energy. We live longer, are less susceptible to the major diseases, and are more likely to recover from those diseases if we get them.

If you were born in, say, 1999, your life expectancy is 79.4 years, whereas your male counterpart's is 73.9 years. According to the World Health Organization, women on average live longer than men in all but two countries in the world. Part of the reason women live longer is that we smoke less, drink less, and take fewer life-threatening chances than men do. But we also tend to be less vulnerable to fatal illnesses like cancer and heart disease. Researchers used to attribute that to the fact that men—who went out to the workplace every day while women stayed home—were under more stress, which is believed to be a contributor to many fatal diseases. But many more women are out in the workforce today than in decades past. In the United States, for example, the number of working women rose from 34 percent in 1950 to 60 percent in 2000, and researchers are finding that working women are just as healthy as those women who stay at home.

It now appears that Mother Nature once again favored women. Scientists point to female hormones as one piece to the puzzle. One of the duties of estrogen, the female hormone, is to keep a woman's blood vessels pliable so they'll be able to accommodate extra blood volume during pregnancy. A happy side benefit of this is that it reduces our risk of developing atherosclerosis, the clogging of the arteries that is the cause of heart disease. Also, because a fetus would need plenty of carbohydrates but little fat, estrogen helps the body to break down excess fat by stimulating the liver to produce HDL (high-density lipoproteins), also known as the good cholesterol. HDL, which enables the body to make more efficient use of fat, also helps to keep the arteries clear of LDL (low-density lipoproteins), also known as the bad cholesterol.

How valuable are these safeguards? Look at the numbers: A twenty-four-year study of the health of nearly six thousand men and women ages thirty to fifty-nine found about twice the incidence of heart disease in the men as in the women, even in the upper age range, where women have less estrogen than their younger counterparts. Before women hit menopause—that is, once they stop having periods for good—we are four times less prone to heart attacks as men are.

Testosterone, the male hormone, seems to be responsible for decreasing a male's HDL, or good cholesterol, while raising his level of LDL, or bad cholesterol. Testosterone, which is responsible for aggressiveness, seems to have "hung on past its glory days," as health writer Edward Dolnick once put it. "[It] may have been a nifty innovation when men's major duty was hurling rocks at the next tribe. But testosterone doesn't seem like a bargain anymore—since today we hunt only if someone has misplaced the remote-control clicker."

Another key factor may be the mounting evidence linking heart disease with the amount of iron a person eats and then stores in the body. Contrary to popular belief—"Eat your meat! It's full of iron to keep you healthy!"—the more iron you store, the higher your risk of a heart attack might be. In fact, one study in Finland of nineteen hundred men showed that high iron levels are second only to smoking when it comes to heart attack risk factors. The typical female of childbearing age has only a third as much iron stored as her male counterpart. Why? Because when we menstruate each month, we lose a significant amount of iron. So, despite the pain and the hassle, what many people used to call "the curse" looks very much like a blessing!

Finally, another advantage Mother Nature bestowed upon females is more body fat. On average, men have 15 percent body fat while women have 23 percent. Fat is the body's fuel, and the 8 percent more that women have stashed away gives us more energy and stamina than men have. And that's one of the major reasons that women survive physically stressful situations, such as being shipwrecked, better than men do and that . . . well, take a quick peek ahead to #42.

Female muscles may not be as strong as male muscles, but they definitely have their advantages.

Male muscles are "striated"—meaning they have a high fiber content. Female muscles are smooth and less fibrous. "[Men's] striated muscles use energy in a less efficient manner than women's," wrote Joe Tanenbaum in *Male and Female Realities: Understanding the Opposite Sex* (1991). "Striated muscles allow immediate use of strength, but burn energy (that is, generate more heat) faster, thereby depleting the body's reserves more quickly." In fact, researchers in Atlanta concluded that just having more muscle mass *period* generates more heat and thus puts males at a disadvantage during contests like marathons. That additional muscle-spawned heat makes men sweat more and therefore causes them to lose sodium and potassium (which play important roles in regulating body processes) faster than women do.

And there's more. Female muscles seem to be more adaptable to changes in the body. "Women's muscles have to adapt to a changing menstrual cycle with varied levels of hormones and water retention at different times of the month," according to *Parents* magazine. "Men's muscles are used to a relatively more stable environment—and so are more easily thrown for a loop when illness strikes, perhaps explaining why men complain of aches and pains more frequently when they get the flu." The magazine added that the muscles of women are less likely to build up pain inducers than those of men. The result? Women may persevere on a task after men have given up because of the pain.

A woman personally led more American slaves to freedom than anyone else.

14

Her name was Harriet Tubman, and she was the most famous and successful "conductor" on the Underground Railroad—the secret routes slaves took from their homes in the South to the free states in the North. An escaped slave herself, Tubman led three hundred slaves to freedom—in nineteen round-trips over ten years—via nighttime treks through swamps and forests that were heavily patrolled by slave catchers who had been lured into the business by the hefty reward the slave owners offered. A $40,000 reward—a fortune in those days—was set on Tubman herself because her feats so enraged southern slave owners. The reward was for her capture dead or alive; had she been caught, she most likely would have been put to death on the spot, and she knew it. She never lost a "passenger."

Nicknamed "Moses" because she, like her biblical counterpart, led her people out of slavery, Tubman served as an unofficial spy/scout for the North during the Civil War. Organizing black troops for the Union Army, she became their commanding officer. On June 2, 1863, she led them on a raid up South Carolina's Combahee River, setting fire to plantations, Confederate warehouses, and arsenals, and freeing another eight hundred slaves plus five hundred prisoners of war along the way. Tubman's planning and execution of the mission were so perfect that not one of her troops was even injured let alone killed.

Tubman accomplished all of this despite the fact that when she was a teenage slave, an overseer threw an iron weight at her for interfering with his capture of an escaping slave, and it fractured Tubman's skull. The injury gave her periodic fainting spells for the rest of her life.

While we're on the subject of the War between the States . . .

More than any other factor, a book written by a woman incited the Civil War, the war that ended slavery in America.

The writer was Harriet Beecher Stowe and the book was *Uncle Tom's Cabin*. When Abraham Lincoln met her during the Civil War, he remarked, "So this is the little lady who started this big war." There's ample evidence that he wasn't kidding.

Stowe, both the daughter and wife of Protestant ministers, first became interested in the issue of slavery when she lived in Cincinnati, a station on the Underground Railroad, and made visits across the Ohio River to Kentucky, a slave state. She saw the slave system in practice on one side of the river and heard the stories of the escaped slaves on the other. That input, along with *An Appeal in Favor of That Class of Americans Called Africans* and other antislavery books and articles in circulation in the North at that time, provided her with a wealth of information from which to draw her fictional characters and plot.

The hero of the overly melodramatic tale, which was first published as a serial in an antislavery newspaper, is the saintly Uncle Tom. In telling his story and the stories of several other slaves, Stowe covered in horrifying detail such realities of slavery as being sold at auction, being separated from one's children, and being forced to have sex. In the book's ending—which Stowe wrote first—Uncle Tom is beaten to death by his cruel master, Simon Legree, because he refuses to provide information about two escaped slaves.

Stowe apparently hoped to *avert* a war with her book. According to letters and other material written by and about her, Stowe's major goal was to reconcile the differences between the North and the South. In a letter she wrote to a friend, she said she hoped that her book would moderate the bitterness of extremist abolitionists. She also wanted to inspire more compassion for blacks throughout the country. Convinced that her main audience would be southerners, she believed she portrayed the South fairly, making sure to include a few kind and compassionate slave owners in the story.

Stowe was stunned when the South reacted to her book with a storm of protest and hatred. She received thousands of furious letters from southerners, including one letter that contained the cut-off ear of a slave. Some southern courts imposed long prison sentences on anyone caught with the book, and numerous southern authors wrote their own books that they claimed presented slavery as it really was.

But more important in the long run was the reaction to the book in the North. By 1860 *Uncle Tom's Cabin*, which had been published in 1851 (and had sold 2.5 million copies worldwide in that first year alone), had turned huge numbers of northerners into rabid haters of slavery and made them ready and willing to go to war over the practice. Author Robert B. Downs, who included *Uncle Tom's Cabin* in his *Books That Changed America*, implies that, at the very least, the book hastened the Civil War by several years. Downs bolsters the argument that the book was in fact a major cause of the war by quoting "loyal Southerner" Thomas Nelson Page, who spent his childhood during the Civil War on a Virginia plantation and was later the U.S. ambassador to Italy and a novelist, who critics said idealized plantation life. According to Page, "By arousing the general sentiment of the world against slavery, the novel contributed more than any other one thing to its abolition in that generation [and] did more than any one thing that ever occurred to precipitate the war."

The book was eventually translated into twenty-three languages. Stowe was visited and lauded by Mark Twain, thanked for her "good work" by England's Queen Victoria, and told that *Uncle Tom's Cabin* was one of the "great achievements of the human mind" by Russian novelist Leo Tolstoy.

Stowe herself put her money where her mouth was. With some of the royalties she earned from the book, she bought slaves and then freed them.

While the Civil War gave black Americans their freedom, it didn't grant them equality. That discrepancy would simmer for nearly a hundred years until . . .

16

The courageous act of one woman triggered the momentous American civil rights movement of the 1960s.

On December 1, 1955, a forty-two-year-old black woman named Rosa Parks boarded a city bus in Montgomery, Alabama. Parks, a seamstress active in the local branch of the National Association for the Advancement of Colored People (NAACP), was weary from her day's work. As required by Alabama's racial segregation laws, she took a seat in the back of the bus; the front was always reserved for whites. Soon the white section was full, and the bus driver "expanded" it to include the row Parks was sitting in. The driver ordered Parks to relinquish her seat to a white man. Parks had argued with bus drivers over this practice in the past, and one time she'd been thrown off a bus because she refused to use the rear door—another requirement. These incidents had given Parks a reputation as a troublemaker among the city's bus drivers, and many would drive right past her without stopping if they saw her standing alone at a bus stop.

On this particular December day, Parks was fed up with the humiliation and unfairness of not just the bus rules but of all of the segregation laws in the South that were designed to keep black people apart from and inferior to whites. She refused to give up her seat. "I knew someone had to take the first step," she later told a reporter.

"I felt it was the right time and opportunity to let it be known that I didn't think I was treated right. If I hadn't done it then, I would have found some other way to make my feelings and desires known."

Parks was arrested for violating segregation laws. Her arrest infuriated local blacks. In response, they staged a bus boycott that lasted for more than a year and nearly bankrupted the bus company. The boycott solidified the black community . . . and also brought a young minister named Martin Luther King, Jr., into the spotlight. The subsequent crusades of King, Parks, and other black activists eventually resulted in the federal Civil Rights Act of 1957, the federal Voting Rights Act of 1965, and several Supreme Court decisions—including one in Parks's case that made bus segregation illegal. Together, these actions put an end to official segregation in the South.

Parks died in 2005. She was the first woman to lie in state (that is, her coffin was displayed at the United States Capitol building). This honor is usually reserved for presidents of the United States.

Women are especially well suited to be doctors.

This is particularly true from a patient's point of view. Women physicians treat their patients more like equals than male doctors do. According to numerous studies, women doctors are more respectful, spend a lot more time with each patient, and interrupt that patient less frequently than their male counterparts. Women just as readily embrace new medical technology and aggressive medical treatments. Adds Mike Adams, who calls himself the Health Ranger, "The best Western doctors I know are all women. . . . They are more caring—and even intuitive—in working to understand what's going on with patients and what therapies might be beneficial to them. Female doctors also tend to be more open to alternative or complementary therapies such as acupuncture, nutritional therapy, or homeopathy."

Continues Adams, in an Internet article entitled "Western Medicine's Domination by Egoistic, Narrow-Minded Male Physicians Now Being Overturned by an Increase in Female Doctors":

> The bottom line to all this is the fact that more females are taking up positions as doctors around the world, and that's actually good news for medicine. We need more women in this profession because we need more open-mindedness, more open communication between physicians and patients, and a more caring attitude about patients at a fundamental level.

And the number of women doctors is, happily, increasing rapidly. Between 1975 and 2005 the percentage of women physicians in the United States tripled—from 9 percent to 25 percent. In 2004, for the first time in history, women made up the majority of medical school applicants. It's been predicted that by 2010 about 40 percent of American physicians will be women.

Geneticist Ann Moir and writer David Jessel, who together wrote *Brain Sex: The Real Difference Between Men and Women*, say that women's "superiority in sensitivity and verbal ability" probably makes us not just better doctors than men but better priests, legislators, and judges as well.

BONUS! Women also make better astronauts.

When former First Lady and current Senator Hillary Rodham Clinton was twelve years old, she supposedly wrote to NASA asking how she could become an astronaut. NASA responded that she did not qualify because of her gender.

If astronauts had been chosen from the start based on their biological qualifications alone, it would have been the *other* gender that couldn't qualify. Why? Because females are smaller, weigh less, need less oxygen and food, are generally healthier, and handle stress better. Also, our eyes are better at distinguishing tiny objects (such as stars) out of a large field (like outer space). You have to wonder why it took till 1983 for the United States to put a woman, Dr. Sally Ride, who had earned a Ph.D. in physics, into space. The Russians were more enlightened on this issue. Cosmonaut Valentina Tereshkova, the first woman in space, piloted the *Vostok 6* spacecraft a full twenty years earlier, in 1963. BTW, Ride is devoted to "empowering girls to explore the world of science—from astrobiology to zoology and everything in between." (Check out her Web site at www.sallyridescience.com.)

A man may have been first to set foot on the moon, but the first human being on Mars just might be a woman. After all, it was a woman, Donna Shirley, who was the manager of the Mars Exploration Program, truly the first successful mission to land spacecraft on Mars. According to one Web site about Shirley: "On July 4, 1997, the entire world watched as the Mars Pathfinder and the Sojourner Rover successfully landed on Mars. Two months later, the Mars Global Surveyor successfully went into orbit around the red planet. Not only were these events two of the U.S. space program's greatest successes, but they may well provide the world with some of the most important scientific data of the twentieth and twenty-first centuries." Shirley was also the original leader of the team that built the Sojourner Rover, which collected data on the makeup of Martian soil and rocks, among other things, and continued to operate twelve times its expected lifetime of seven days.

P.S. We also invented the space suit.

Women have written many of our most enduring and influential books.

Take Louisa May Alcott's *Little Women* (1868), whose brave and brainy Jo March was a hundred years ahead of her time.

Other standouts: Emily Brontë's tale of the ultimate dysfunctional relationship in the passionate *Wuthering Heights* (1847), and her sister Charlotte's *Jane Eyre* (also published in 1847), the story of a Cinderella with guts. Jane Austen wrote *Pride and Prejudice* (1813); Mary Ann Evans (writing under the name George Eliot!) penned *The Mill on the Floss* (1860) and *Silas Marner* (1861). Swiss writer Johanna Spyri was praised for her "insight into a child's mind" when she published *Heidi* in 1880. Edith Wharton wrote *Ethan Frome* (1911) and *The Age of Innocence* (1920), both of which became movies of the 1990s.

A woman, Margaret Mitchell, created the most popular heroine in American fiction, Scarlett O'Hara, in *Gone with the Wind* (1936), and Harriet Beecher Stowe, who wrote the antislavery novel *Uncle Tom's Cabin*, probably incited the American Civil War (see #15), the war that altered Scarlett's life—and Scarlett herself—forever.

In 1934 P. L. Travers began her *Mary Poppins* series, creating a character "who proved that you can be an independent, strong-willed, authoritarian woman without being a bitch," according to a former screenwriter for Disney, the studio that turned the series into a wildly successful movie in 1964.

Pearl Buck was awarded a 1932 Pulitzer Prize (one of the highest awards in literature) for *The Good Earth* about a poor Chinese couple and their struggle to achieve wealth. Other Pulitzer Prize winners were Harper Lee (in 1961) for *To Kill a Mockingbird*, an early plea for racial justice; and (posthumously) Anne Frank, who in her diary had written of her hope of living on after her death through her writing, but who certainly couldn't have imagined the scope to which she would do just that.

Betty Friedan's book *The Feminist Mystique* (1963) is widely credited with starting the modern feminist movement. In the book, Friedan revealed the emptiness and frustration of many American women in their traditional roles. She cofounded NOW (the National Organization for Women) in 1966, and throughout that decade and beyond, she urged women "to do something to visibly protest the discrimination against women."

And let us, of course, pay homage to J. K. Rowling and her Harry Potter series. The first book in the series, *Harry Potter and the Sorcerer's Stone*, is the third best-selling book *ever*, coming in behind the Bible and *The Quotations of Chairman Mao Tse Tung* (which the Chinese people were kind of forced to own). Rowling is a billionaire and believed to be richer than England's Queen Elizabeth. And although many adults have a problem with the witchcraft elements in the books, the fact remains that Harry is responsible for getting a whole generation of kids interested in reading books.

Incidentally, the first-ever novel, *The Tale of Genji*, was written by a woman, Lady Murasaki Shikibu, in eleventh-century Japan.

It was thanks to the efforts of a woman that most Americans obtained the right to vote.

ere's how the Organization for Equal Education of the Sexes (OEES) explains it: While George Washington helped win the vote for fewer than two million white men and Abraham Lincoln helped win the vote for fewer than one million black men, Susan B. Anthony helped win the vote for twenty-six million American women. Although she wasn't among those who made the *first* demand for votes for women (which happened in 1848), and she wasn't alive to see women finally cast ballots in a national election in 1920, no one worked harder than Anthony to win that right. From 1851 until she died in 1906, she made this cause her only employment and the main focus of her life, according to the OEES. Her energy, determination, and executive ability are what held together the suffrage movement—which was subject to much of its own political infighting—for more than fifty years.

Anthony was born in 1820 into a Quaker community, which in those days treated women with far more equality than the rest of society. She set her sights on a teaching career and spent ten years in the profession, earning $2.50 a week. After growing dissatisfied with teaching—and full of outrage that male teachers earned significantly more money—Anthony quit and turned her attention to politics. She became active in the temperance (anti-alcohol) and antislavery movements. In the course of this work, she met Elizabeth Cady Stanton, who would become her primary partner in the long quest for the right to vote.

When they met, Stanton was already active in the women's rights movement, having organized the first American women's rights convention in Seneca Falls, New York, in 1848. She had little trouble converting Anthony to her cause, since Anthony had experienced so much discrimination herself, not just as a teacher but in the temperance movement as well. At temperance conventions, as at teachers meetings, women were not allowed to express their opinions before the crowd.

The collaboration of Anthony and Stanton was perfect. Stanton was an accomplished writer, and Anthony became a powerful and effective public speaker of Stanton's words. As Stanton's husband, Henry, once expressed it to his wife: "You stir up Susan and she stirs up the world."

Anthony was also fantastically successful at recruiting others to the cause and then inspiring them to work for it as doggedly as she did. Anthony herself was able to work ceaselessly because she was unmarried and childless, unlike Stanton who had seven children.

In 1868 Anthony and Stanton began publishing a weekly newspaper (the *Revolution*) devoted to the women's rights battle, and in 1869 they founded the first American organization (the National Woman Suffrage Association) devoted solely to getting the vote for women. Anthony then spent the next thirty years on the road, keeping to an exhausting schedule of meetings and lectures—at which most of the audience had never before heard a woman speak in public—designed to win converts to her cause. Averaging seventy-five to one hundred speeches a year, she did, in fact, change the national attitude about votes for women. In 1878 Anthony's friend, Senator A. A. Sargent of California, introduced into Congress the Susan B. Anthony Amendment, which would grant women the right to vote throughout the United States. But because most politicians were nowhere near as enlightened as Sargent, the amendment would not become law for another forty-two years.

Long before that, Anthony died. Did she die full of self-pity that she would not live to see women get the right she had fought so long for? No way. She died full of optimism. Shortly before her friend and colleague Stanton died in 1902, Anthony wrote to her about the younger, more radical generation of suffragists emerging on the scene and assured Stanton that she had "not a shadow of a doubt that they will carry our cause to victory." And just three weeks before her own death in 1906, a seriously ill Anthony—she'd had a stroke—made a speech at the annual suffrage convention, in which she asserted: "I have never lost my faith, not for a moment. Failure is impossible."

And she was right. The Susan B. Anthony Amendment was signed into law in 1920, exactly one hundred years after Anthony was born.

Only a woman can be the First Lady of the United States.

Yeah, right, we know . . . some consolation for there never having been a female president, huh? Well, there *will* be a woman president in your lifetime . . . and a First Gentleman, probably, as well.

The fact is, though, First Ladies have come to have more power and influence over the past fifty years or so. The job requires a lot more than just doing a queenly wave while walking across the grass with the president and playing hostess at state dinners for foreign dignitaries and such.

Eleanor Roosevelt, the wife of President Franklin D. Roosevelt, was the first to change the role of the president's wife forever. In 1933 she held her first press conference, allowing only women reporters to attend (rah!). After that and even after her husband died in office, she worked ceaselessly for human rights, civil rights, and women's rights, and for the poor and unemployed. In 1945 she was named U.S. Delegate to the United Nations, where she played a major role in helping to pass the Universal Declaration of Human Rights. In 1961 President John F. Kennedy named her as chair of the Commission on the Status of Women. Former First Lady and now Senator Hillary Rodham Clinton once said that Eleanor Roosevelt was her favorite role model.

Many of the greatest reforms to the American way of life were instigated by women.

Just a few examples:

In the mid-1800s a teacher named Dorothea Dix volunteered to teach a Sunday school class at a prison and was horrified to discover that mentally ill people were imprisoned along with criminals because there was nowhere else to keep them. She embarked on a ten-year crusade to reform the U.S. penal system and the care of the mentally ill. Traveling some thirty thousand miles, she visited hundreds of state prisons and city jails, lectured widely, drafted legislation, worked with state legislatures in nearly every state, and provided a detailed program for reform. She also worked to make treatment more constructive and humane at mental institutions. There were only thirteen such facilities when Dix began her crusade. By 1880 there were one hundred twenty-three, thanks to her efforts, and she had personally designed and founded thirty-five of them. She also took her ideas abroad, sparking reform in country after country she visited.

Also in the 1800s, sisters Sarah and Angelina Grimke—white women who grew up on a South Carolina slave plantation—were leaders in the movement to abolish slavery, along with Elizabeth Cady Stanton and Lucretia Mott. Once that was accomplished, all four went on to prominence in America's first women's rights movement, in which women sought such basic freedoms as being allowed to vote, to attend college, to get custody of their children after a divorce, to keep their own earnings, and to own property. Before the Civil War, the legal status of an American wife was comparable to that of a slave in the South.

In 1871, a few years after she lost her husband and all four of her children to an epidemic of yellow fever and then lost her dressmaking business in the great Chicago fire, Mary Harris Jones became obsessed with the plight of American workers. In many industries, wages were piddling and working conditions were deplorable and dangerous. For the next fifty years, despite being mobbed, beaten, and imprisoned, Mother Jones (as she became known) organized workers, especially miners, into fledgling labor unions that pushed for improved pay and working conditions.

In the last years of the nineteenth century, Jane Addams, a woman from a wealthy family, became appalled at the conditions of the city slums, which were teeming with immigrants. Some of her complaints, in her own words: "Unsanitary housing, poisonous sewage, contaminated water, infant mortality, the spread of contagion, adulterated food, impure milk, smoke-laden air, ill-ventilated factories, dangerous occupations, juvenile crime, [and] unwholesome crowding. . . ." She decided to borrow the British idea of "settlement houses" for America and established one in Chicago. Her Hull House became the model for settlement houses all over the world. Settlement house workers helped immigrants become established in America by, for example, teaching them English. But they also pressured city administrators to improve conditions in the slums by providing health and sanitation programs, and they campaigned against the sweatshop system and many of the other causes of poverty in the slums. Addams was in essence responsible for ushering in a national movement for enlightened and drastically needed social welfare policies. In 1931 Jane Addams became the first woman to win the Nobel Peace Prize for her work with the poor in Chicago.

Florence Kelley, who often worked with Jane Addams, could be called the mother of the consumer protection movement, which thrives to this day. Kelley was executive secretary of the National Consumers League for thirty-two years. She not only demanded and got consumer protection laws but also worked feverishly through educational campaigns and boycotts against the exploitation of workers, particularly working children. Children as young as six were toiling in canneries, mines, and airless mills. They were frequently injured or killed on the job. And they were grossly underpaid. In the sewing sweatshops, for example, they made only about four cents an hour. The League's pioneering efforts eventually resulted in the Fair Labor Standards Act of 1938, which abolished child labor.

Margaret Sanger—a public health nurse whose mother bore eleven children and died at age forty-eight—led a decades-long fight to abolish laws that made it illegal for doctors to distribute birth control devices or even information on how women could limit the number of children they had. Sanger believed that being forced to bear numerous children seriously undermined a woman's health and was a major contributing factor to poverty. In defiance of the law, Sanger opened the first birth control clinic in the United States in 1916.

The clinic was located in a poor section of Brooklyn, and more than one hundred fifty women waited in line the day it opened. Later, a sweatshop worker who already had eight children would plead, "If you don't help me, I'll chop up a glass and swallow it tonight!" Police arrested Sanger and shut down the clinic on its tenth day of operation. Though Sanger encountered strong opposition year after year—and was jailed at least nine times for her efforts—she lived to see the dispensing of birth control information and devices legalized in the United States in 1937.

Women also sparked reform by introducing readers to the horrible lives of downtrodden Americans through fiction. Harriet Beecher Stowe's *Uncle Tom's Cabin*, for example, roused into action northerners who had been indifferent about slavery (see #15). Elizabeth S. Phelps Ward's 1871 *The Silent Partner* detailed inhumane factory conditions. *Ramona*, authored by Helen Hunt Jackson and published in 1884, was an impassioned account of the plight of American Indians and a plea for justice.

Dolores Huerta was a teacher who was dismayed to see the effects of working conditions on migrant workers' families when children came to school barefoot and hungry. She left teaching to work on their behalf. In 1962, with Cesar Chavez, she cofounded the United Farm Workers (UFW) union in California. Her efforts led to the passage of the Agricultural Labor Relations Act of 1975. It was the first "bill of rights" for farm workers in the United States. "I thought I could do more by organizing farm workers than by trying to teach their hungry children," she once said.

The late Doris Tate, whose daughter, actress Sharon Tate and several others were murdered by the Manson Family in 1969, is considered the mother of the victims' rights movement. She was the first relative in the state of California to speak before a parole board at a hearing for one of her daughter's murderers. She campaigned vigorously to make that privilege a law. Thanks to Tate, it is now a law in all fifty American states that victims and their families are entitled to speak at trials and parole hearings.

Rising above discouragement from white teachers and classmates, Winona LaDuke began to speak out at an early age about the disproportionate difficulties faced by her fellow Native Americans, including the terrible pollution on reservations. Eventually, she went to Harvard to study environmental issues and was the youngest person ever to address the United Nations. At age twenty-nine, she won the Reebok Human Rights Award. She founded the White Earth Land Recovery Project at her tribe's White Earth Reservation in Minnesota. Her project fights poverty and pollution by reclaiming treaty lands. Her efforts were so admired that she was the U.S. Green Party's vice presidential candidate in the 1996 and 2000 national elections. According to one writer, "Her achievements show young readers the positive impact of one person's determination to change her own world."

To end on a lighter note, the wildly popular U.S. cooking show host Rachael Ray was placed on *Time* magazine's 2006 "World's Most Influential People" list. According to *Time*, Ray has inspired working people to "eschew the trap of fast-food facility and truly cook—even the easy fast stuff—at home."

21

Many of the most recent reforms in the world were made by women.

T hese women won the Nobel Peace Prize, probably the most prestigious award on the planet:

* Betty Williams and Máiread Corrigan, Northern Ireland, 1976. These two advocates of nonviolence made a dramatic effort to resolve the longstanding violent conflict between the Catholics and the Protestants in their country. They met shortly after Corrigan's niece and two nephews were killed as a result of violence between the two groups.

* Aung San Suu Kyi, Myanmar (formerly Burma), 1991. She received the award for her nonviolent struggle for democracy and human rights in her country. She became the leader of a democratic opposition that employed nonviolent means to resist a regime characterized by brutality. The Nobel Committee wanted to honor "her efforts to show its support for the many people throughout the world who are striving to attain democracy, human rights, and ethnic conciliation by peaceful means."

* Rigoberta Menchú, Guatemala, 1992. Like many other countries in South and Central America, Guatemala has experienced great tension between the descendants of European immigrants and the native Indian population. In the 1970s and 1980s that ten-

sion came to a head in the large-scale repression of Indian peoples. Menchú played a prominent role as an advocate of native rights.

❋ Shirin Ebadi, Iran, 2003. Ebadi is a Muslim and a lawyer, judge, lecturer, writer, and activist. As the Nobel Committee put it, "she has spoken out clearly and strongly in her country, Iran, and far beyond its borders. She has stood up as a sound professional, a courageous person, and has never heeded the threats to her own safety." In her efforts to achieve democracy and to fight for human rights, she has focused especially on the rights of women and children.

Another great reformer is Ela Bhatt of India. She overcame her shyness and her stuttering to start a union, the Self-Employed Women's Association, for the poorest women in India. She listened to their concerns and helped them implement their ideas. The result? They started a bank, worker cooperatives, child care cooperatives, and an insurance program.

Mamphela Ramphele of South Africa overcame gender and race prejudice to become a medical doctor. She worked alongside some of the most prominent leaders in South Africa to end the practice of apartheid—that is, the separation of whites and blacks.

22

Women actually behave much better than men when it comes to truly frightening situations.

This one should neatly quash any taunt along the lines of "Girls are such scaredy-cats!" True, girls are more likely than boys to scream or run when they see a mouse or spider, mainly because people don't admonish or make fun of girls for showing fear as they do boys. But when it comes to the truly big scary stuff—such as an earthquake or a tornado—adult women are much better able than men to cope and function. Many studies support this, including an important one conducted during World War II that showed that in the heavily bombed residential areas of London and Kent, 70 percent more men than women broke down and needed psychiatric help. Another source says that under blockade, bombardment, and concentration camp conditions during the two world wars, more men were psychiatric casualties at a ratio of seventy to one. As author/editor/publisher Leonard Woolf (the husband of British author and early feminist Virginia Woolf) once observed, "With or without screaming, women in dangerous situations are more apt to turn and do something, while men seem to lapse into a catatonic state."

Females not only cope better with *emotional* pain . . .

Doctors agree that females bear physical pain far better than males do.

This is pretty impressive when you consider that because females are more "tactilely sensitive" than males we feel pain more acutely than they do.

Why are females better at enduring pain? The theory: It's Mother Nature's way of preparing us for labor and delivery.

At any rate, as Theo Lang suggested in *The Difference Between a Man and a Woman*: "The exhortation commonly addressed to an injured weeping boy 'Be a man!' might be better phrased 'Be a woman!'"

Women instituted early-childhood education in the United States.

While visiting Germany in 1871, Susan Blow of St. Louis became acquainted with and fell in love with the kindergarten program designed by the late German educator Friedrich Froebel. Froebel had coined the term *kindergarten*—which translates as "children's garden"—to convey the impression that in this type of class young children could grow freely like plants in a garden as they participated in a set routine of organized games, songs, and stories, plus gardening and other constructive work.

An enthusiastic Blow returned to St. Louis and convinced William T. Harris, then superintendent of the city's schools, to let her introduce kindergarten into the school system. To prepare herself for the task, Blow went to New York City in 1872 to further study kindergarten methods with Maria Kraus-Boelte, a student of Froebel's widow. When Blow returned to St. Louis in 1873, she opened the first public-school kindergarten in America at the Des Peres School. (The first *private* kindergarten in America had been established years earlier—in 1855—in Wisconsin. But it, too, was founded by a woman, Margaretha Meyer Schurz.)

In 1874 Blow opened a training school for kindergarten teachers and saw her innovation take off in popularity. By 1880 kindergartens had become fixtures throughout the St. Louis school system, and the concept was spreading across the United States. By the turn of the century the United States counted 225,494 kindergartners (58 percent of whom attended kindergarten in public schools).

In the 1920s and 1930s more and more American women entered the labor market so that nursery schools (now primarily known as preschools), which seized upon and simplified many of the kindergarten methods for use with three- and four-year-olds, also increased in popularity. The first nursery school in America had also been founded by a woman, Joanna Bethune. A teacher who had done extensive charity work among the poor in New York City, Bethune founded the Infant School Society in 1827 and a few months later opened the first "infant school," designed for children eighteen months to five years old. She intended the school to provide a little child-care relief for working parents. Soon Bethune was supervising nine such schools throughout New York City, and another innovation in early childhood education was spreading across America.

Incidentally, historians and educators credit yet another woman— Dr. Maria Montessori—with having had enormous influence on the evolution of the nursery school over the years. Montessori, an Italian physician and teacher, did not like the way traditional European classes were so dominated by the teacher. Children had little opportunity to learn on their own. So she devised games, methods, and materials to encourage children between two and five to do it themselves—be it vocabulary building or motor-skill development—while the teacher remained in the background. Her books, including *The Montessori Method* (1912), have been widely read by teachers for generations.

And we cannot leave a discussion about the spectacular achievements of women in early childhood education without mentioning Joan Ganz Cooney, who in 1969 created a place called Sesame Street. Cooney, who had been producing public television documentaries in New York City, was a pioneer in tapping television as an educational resource for kids. "If this country can get a man on the moon," she said in those days, "surely we should be able to figure out how to use this instrument for the betterment of society." She had become aware that while children from middle-class homes arrived on the first day of kindergarten already knowing their numbers and letters, disadvantaged kids didn't. She designed *Sesame Street* to bring these poorer kids up to par through humor, music, and great graphics. But middle-class kids also became enchanted with the program, and that doesn't bother Cooney one bit. "It was always meant to help all kids," she said in an interview on the occasion of the show's twentieth anniversary. "But the disadvantaged kids were the bull's-eye of the target."

Has *Sesame Street* done its job? There's been some argument about this over the years. The program has been accused, for example, of achieving little more than "rote memorization"—that is, a memorizing process using repetition and little thought—and of teaching children "to read not books but television." But a number of studies carried out since the early 1970s have consistently shown that kids who watch the show have a marked improvement in thinking skills over those who don't. And so many millions of kids watch it that, shortly after the show went on the air, the kindergarten curriculum had to be upgraded. Child and adolescent psychiatrist David Fassler once remarked in *Healthy Kids* magazine, "Kids come to preschool and first grade with a much more developed sense of knowledge, which they appear to have acquired through *Sesame Street*."

So long live Big Bird, Bert and Ernie, Elmo . . . and their mom.

P.S. *Barney*, starring a dinosaur who's been called "the Elvis for toddlers," was also created by women: Sheryl Leach and Kathy Parker. (Come on, admit it, at one time you *loved* Barney.) Valerie Walsh was a cocreator of *Dora the Explorer*, and Traci Paige Johnson and Angela Santomero were two of the three creators of *Blue's Clues*.

Girls have a big advantage over boys on timed tests.

In a recently released study of more than eight thousand males and females ranging in age from two to ninety from across the United States, Vanderbilt University researchers Stephen Camarata and Richard Woodcock discovered that females have a significant advantage over males on timed tests and tasks. They found that the differences were particularly significant among preteens and teens. "We found very minor differences in overall intelligence," Camarata says. The difference, though, is that females have a faster processing speed—that is, the ability to effectively, efficiently, and accurately complete work that is of moderate difficulty.

"It is very important for teachers to understand this difference in males and females when it comes to assigning work and structuring tests," according to Camarata. "To truly understand a person's overall ability, it is important to also look at performance in un-timed situations. For males, this means presenting them with material that is challenging and interesting, but is presented in smaller chunks without strict time limits."

Girls hear better than boys.

Especially in the higher ranges—high as in soprano—of sound. We're more sensitive to *louder* sounds too. When a noise is 85 decibels or above, it sounds twice as loud to us as it does to guys, which explains why they can crank the music up to full blast and still do their homework. Ironically, however, most females can tolerate much more noise and show fewer ill effects than males can, according to research. We're also better at noticing small changes in volume, which explains "women's superior sensitivity to that 'tone of voice' which their male partners are so often accused of adopting," writes geneticist Anne Moir and writer David Jessel in their book *Brain Sex: The Real Difference Between Men and Women.* And we have better auditory memory—that is, we are better at remembering what we hear. Some experts believe that's why so many more females than males can sing in tune (see #2).

We have better hearing, say Moir and Jessel, because the female brain is organized to respond more sensitively to all sensory stimuli, and that includes not just sound but taste, touch, and smell as well.

26

A woman won more medals and tournaments and set more records in more sports than any other athlete—male or female—in the twentieth century.

She was Mildred "Babe" Didrikson Zaharias, she lived from 1914 to 1956, and she was a superstar in every sport she competed in. Nicknamed Babe because people believed her ability was on a par with Babe Ruth, she first gained attention as a basketball star at her Texas high school, then spent two years on the nationally famous women's basketball team of the Employers Casualty Company in Dallas. Meanwhile, she was also breaking track and field records and winning swimming and figure-skating medals. In the 1932 Olympics she won gold medals in the 80-meter hurdle, then broke the javelin record by 14 feet, and would have done even better than that had her hand not slipped on the javelin.

On that same Olympics trip, she tried golf for the first time, won her first game (against three sports reporters), and became passionate about the sport. Didrikson won the U.S.A. National Women's Championship by the biggest margin ever in 1946 and went on to take 17 straight golf titles in 1947. Despite the fact that she had cancer surgery in 1953, Zaharias won the U.S. Women's Open in 1954.

She excelled at every sport she ever tried—and there's more: She set the women's record for throwing a baseball (296 feet), was one of the best field place kickers in the United States, trained as a boxer, was a top-notch diver and lacrosse player, and toured with the National Exhibition Billiards Team.

Incidentally, Zaharias's skills weren't limited to the playing field. The phenomenal Babe was a featured harmonica soloist on a Texas radio station at the age of seven, and she also sang and played harmonica in vaudeville shows as an adult.

BONUS! Girls walk faster than boys.

The average woman walks 256 feet per minute, whereas the average man does 245 feet, according to *Harper's Index*.

It was a woman who first exposed the harm humans were doing to the environment, igniting the world's environmental movement.

In the late 1950s an eminent marine biologist named Rachel Carson began to collect facts about what pesticides were *really* doing. Instead of just killing bugs on plants, as these chemicals were intended to do, they were also poisoning the plants themselves, the air, the water, and the land, and killing birds, fish, and probably humans as well. "These chemicals are now stored in the vast majority of human beings, regardless of age," Carson wrote. (Decades later, in 1993, a chemist, Mary S. Wolff, would release a study showing that women with the highest exposure to DDT, one of the most popular and deadly pesticides, had four times the risk of breast cancer than women with the least exposure.)

In 1962 Carson published her warnings and the facts that supported them in a book called *Silent Spring*, a title she chose because she feared that if indiscriminant use of toxic chemicals continued, we'd never again hear birds sing because all of them would be dead.

The book, which became an instant best-seller, alarmed the public. People joined in a grass roots campaign to put an end to reckless pesticide use. Legislation was passed to ban the use of DDT, which led to its being banned in many other countries as well. And magazines like *Time* and *Newsweek* began to regularly cover environmental damage—and not just from pesticides—that was occurring all over the world.

Carson died of cancer in 1964. She did not live to see just how big the environmental revolution she had started would become. In 1970, for example, the United States would create the federal Environmental Protection Agency. And on April 22 of that year, millions of Americans would demonstrate against pollution to mark the very first Earth Day.

But Rachel Carson died happy. "I had said I could never again listen happily to a thrush song if I had not done all I could," she had written to a friend. "And last night the thoughts of all the birds and other creatures and all the loveliness that is in nature came to me with such a surge of deep happiness, now that I had done what I could."

Many other women have been pioneers or have played important roles in the environmental movement. Among them is Dr. Sylvia Earle, former chief scientist at the U.S. National Oceanic and Atmospheric Administration, a distinguished marine biologist, and a veteran of more than six thousand hours of underwater study. She wrote the book *Sea Change: A Message of the Oceans* (1995), which has been described "as a Rachel Carson–like plea for the preservation of the oceans."

Similarly, *Time* magazine said that *China's Water Crisis* (1999), written by former journalist Ma Jun, "may be for China what Rachel Carson's *Silent Spring* was for the United States, the country's first great environmental call to arms." The magazine listed her among the 2006 "World's Top 100 Most Influential People."

Karen Silkwood, a chemical technician in the early 1970s at the Kerr-McGee plutonium fuels production plant in Crescent City, Oklahoma, was an activist who was critical of the plant's safety. She was one of the first to sound the alarm about the dangers of plutonium exposure. In the weeks before her death in 1974 she was gathering evidence for her union, the Oil, Chemical, and Atomic Workers' Union, to support her claim that the company she worked for was negligent in maintaining plant safety. She died in a mysterious one-car crash. Meryl Streep played the title role in the 1983 movie *Silkwood* about Karen Silkwood's efforts.

In 1978 Lois Gibbs, a stay-at-home mom with two kids, started wondering if her children's unusual health problems, as well as those of her neighbors in Niagara Falls, New York, were connected to their exposure to leaking chemical waste. She discovered that her neighborhood had been built on top of 21,000 tons of buried chemical waste, which became known as the Love Canal. Gibbs started a grass roots effort against the local, state, and federal governments. It took years, but thanks to Gibbs and her organization, more than eight hundred families were evacuated, and the cleanup of the Love Canal began. Thanks to her efforts, the U.S. Environmental Protection Agency created a Superfund, which is used to locate and clean up toxic sites. She is the founder and executive director of the Center for Health, Environment, and Justice (CHEJ), which helps people throughout the United States solve the toxic waste problems in their communities.

In the 1990s Erin Brockovich, an unemployed divorced mom, became a legal assistant and almost single-handedly brought down Pacific Gas and Electric, who she accused of polluting the water supply in Hinkley, California. Her hard work culminated in a $333 million settlement in damages to more than six hundred Hinkley residents who had been affected over the decades by their exposure to the toxic chemical Chromium 6. Julia Roberts won an Oscar for Best Actress for her portrayal of Brockovich in the 2000 movie *Erin Brockovich*.

In 2004 Wangari Maathai of Kenya became the first African woman to win the Nobel Peace Prize, one of the world's most distinguished honors. She had founded the Green Belt Movement in her country in 1977. The group has planted more than thirty million trees to prevent soil erosion and water pollution and to provide firewood for cooking. A United Nations report once ominously reported that only nine trees were being replanted in Africa for every one hundred that were cut down. The Green Belt program has primarily been carried out by Kenyan village women, who believe that by protecting their environment and being paid for their labor, they are able to better care for their children and their children's futures. Maathai's methods have been adopted by other countries as well. The Green Belt Movement also focuses on education, family planning, nutrition, and the fight against corruption. According to the Nobel Committee, "Maathai is a strong voice speaking for the best forces in Africa to promote peace and good living conditions on that continent."

Another pro-forest advocate is Marina Silva of Brazil, who

believes that bulldozing Brazil's rain forest for development of buildings destroys natural resources needed by Brazil and the whole world. Working her way up from a childhood of poverty to become a Brazilian senator, she successfully legislated rain forest preservation to protect her people against poverty and safeguard their way of life.

Girls and women commit far fewer crimes than boys and men.

Here are a few statistics. In the United States in 2003, men committed 81.5 percent of violent crimes (such as rape, robbery, and assault). Women make up 8.5 percent of the prison population in America. This lopsidedness occurs all over the world. According to NationMaster.com (which is, BTW, a great homework source, with tons of international statistics), the percentage of women versus men in prison is highest in Thailand, where women are 20.3 percent of the prison population, and lowest in Sudan, Tuvalu (formerly the Ellice Islands in the Pacific Ocean), Seychelles, and Liechtenstein, where the percentage is zero. The world average is 4.4 percent.

So what's with that? Why do so many more men do the crime and do the time? Researchers believe the answer has both biological and environmental components. Males are born with greater potential for violence because they have far more testosterone, the male hormone that has proved to be the source of aggressive behavior. According to Dr. Myriam Miedzian, higher levels of testosterone create a lower threshold for frustration, more irritability and impatience, greater impulsiveness, a tendency to rough and tumble, and perhaps a greater concern with dominance, "all of which," she says in her book *Boys Will Be Boys: Breaking the Link Between Masculinity and Violence* (2002), "can easily be precursors of violence."

But testosterone alone does not breed violent males, according to Miedzian and other experts. It's society that does that. As anthropologist Ashley Montagu was quoted in the book *The Human Animal*, "Every human being comes into this world loving and trustful and devoid of violent aggression. A violent society like ours creates violent people by warping its children with lessons in violence. Children in societies have their love and trust crippled or destroyed by the institutionalized, approved role models for males that teach them to be aggressive, competitive, and violent." Like the "Terminator" (who, today, is California's Governor). "If human beings are to survive in a nuclear age," according to Miedzian, "committing acts of violence may eventually have to become as embarrassing as urinating or defecating in public."

So role models are one thing. Other research has suggested that the root of most violent crime may be the tendency of males to deny their feelings when they are depressed. In *Boys Will Be Boys*, Miedzian also points to the fact that boys are much more likely to have certain physical disabilities—such as Attention Deficit/Hyperactivity Disorder (ADHD)—that put them at greater risk for behaving violently.

Finally worth noting is the theory—corroborated by several studies and sources—that violence in men can be linked to the fact that they don't give birth to children, nor have they traditionally taken a major role in rearing them. Retired Rutgers University psychologist Dr. Dorothy Dinnerstein, like the eminent anthropologist Margaret Mead, believes that men suffer from "womb envy"—frustration at being unable to give birth to children. As a result, men feel that if their contribution to the world can't be to *create* someone, it will be to *do* something. That, plus the male's innate aggressiveness, has led to a lot of constructive achievements, according to Dinnerstein, but it can go the other way as well. "If you don't have the sense of efficacy [capableness] that comes from helping another human being," she was quoted in *The Human Animal*, "making it possible for another human being to become human, to join the human condition, to change from a helpless infant into a competent child—if you don't have that power" you're more likely to want to go out and impose your will on other people—to hurt, rape, even kill them. Miedzian explains it another way: To raise a child, she says, one must learn considerable patience, nurturance, and empathy—and when qualities like those increase, studies have shown that violence decreases.

Women made two of the earliest and greatest discoveries of our time in genetics—the study of what makes each living thing unique.

Genetic scientist Barbara McClintock spent decades alone in a field on Long Island, New York, studying Indian corn as it grew. In the late 1940s, as a result of her observations, she proposed a theory that set prevailing scientific theory on its ear: Inherited characteristics are *not* logical and predictable, she said. To put it more technically, McClintock asserted that genes—the units on chromosomes by which hereditary characteristics are transmitted and determined— aren't fixed on the chromosomes in permanent locations. Instead, they can jump from one position to another in unpredictable ways. This discovery explains how an organism can adapt and change in future generations; it's how bacteria can become resistant to antibiotics, for example, and how once-normal cells turn into cancer cells.

Unfortunately, the scientific community scoffed at McClintock's finding for years. But that didn't faze her. "If you know you are on the right track, if you have this inner knowledge, then nobody can turn you off," she said in Allen L. Hammond's book *A Passion to Know* (1984). And she was eventually vindicated. In 1983, when she was eighty-one, McClintock was awarded the Nobel Prize for medicine.

The Nobel Committee called McClintock's "jumping genes" theory "one of the two great discoveries of our time in genetics."

And the other great discovery, according to the committee? It was when scientists determined the structure of DNA, the acid in each cell responsible for telling the cell—and ultimately the entire organism or individual—what to look like. Credit for this is traditionally given to James Watson, Francis Crick, and Maurice Wilkins (they won a Nobel Prize in 1962), but they could not have done it without biophysicist Rosalind Franklin. Wilkins was Franklin's supervisor in a research lab at London's Kings College, and it was there that she managed to get the first successful X-ray diffraction picture of the DNA molecule. Wilkins showed this to his friends Watson and Crick, who were stalled in their own research. Using Franklin's photo and some of their own calculations and findings, they went on to build the first DNA model. Why didn't Franklin get any credit for her crucial role in all this? Only the fact that she didn't get in on the Nobel Prize can be satisfactorily explained: Nobel Prizes are awarded only to *living* persons, and Franklin died of cancer—bitter about her lack of recognition—in 1958 at the age of thirty-seven.

A woman was responsible for still another enormously important genetic discovery. In 1905 biologist and geneticist Nettie Stevens, who had been studying a certain kind of beetle, was the first to demonstrate that sex is determined by a particular chromosome. She identified the X and Y chromosomes and showed that the XX combination produces a female and the XY a male. Before that, scientists had believed that external factors like temperature and the food that was eaten determined the sex of offspring of the lower forms of life, such as the beetle, and that divine intervention determined it in humans.

Unfortunately, this is another discovery for which a male scientist—Edmund B. Wilson—traditionally gets the credit. He was conducting similar research at the same time Stevens was and published his findings during the same year. Interestingly, however, in his initial report he said that his findings were "in agreement with the observations of Stevens," which seems to prove that she made the discovery first. In addition, according to the authors of *Mothers of Invention*, Wilson "couldn't or wouldn't be as specific as Stevens in defining these actual X and Y chromosomes" in that first paper, though a few years later—after Stevens died of cancer in 1912—he duplicated and confirmed her findings.

Girls get fewer viral and bacterial illnesses than boys do.

Not only are we less susceptible to the major diseases (see #13), but we get fewer colds, flus, strep throats, and other such bugs. We're simply better at producing the antibodies that fight these invading viruses and bacteria. Why? Researchers suspect it's because we have two X chromosomes in our genetic makeup, whereas males have one X and one Y, and it's the X that carries many of the genes that control immunity. In essence, we have double protection. If something goes wrong with our first X, our bodies can turn to the second for help in fighting infections. Males have no such recourse. For this same reason males are overwhelmingly more likely to be born with conditions like hemophilia and color blindness. These conditions are carried on the X chromosome and in women are almost always counteracted by the other X.

Fewer girls than boys get acne.

It's because males have more testosterone, the hormone that stimulates the sebaceous gland to produce more of the oil that clogs pores and leads to pimples.

And hey, we can much more easily camouflage the zits we do get. With makeup, of course. While makeup on men has become acceptable in a couple of career fields in a couple of big cities, the vast majority of men consider it strictly off-limits to them.

Yes, a man can grow a beard to hide a broken-out chin, but such an addition is hot and scratchy, cannot simply be washed off at the end of the day, and must be checked frequently during meals for the presence of gross food particles. Nor will a beard cover a pimply nose or forehead.

A woman founded the largest organization in the United States.

31

She was Dr. Ethel Percy Andrus and it was the American Association of Retired Persons, which is now simply called AARP. The organization has more than 35 million members. Membership in AARP is open to anyone age fifty or more (and you don't have to be retired to join). With 25 percent of the U.S. population in the over-fifty category, nearly half of all people in this age bracket are AARP members. One out of ten Americans belongs to the organization.

The AARP began as the National Retired Teachers Association (NRTA) in 1947. Andrus, a retired high school principal, founded the NRTA because she was a crusader. As the leader of the NRTA, she fought the California state legislature for pension reform for retired teachers and the U.S. Congress for tax benefits for them. Soon she turned her attention to the greatest fear of retirees at that time: What would happen to them if they sustained a major injury or became gravely ill and required lengthy hospitalization? The problem: In those days, no insurance company would provide health insurance for a person older than sixty-five.

Eventually Andrus, with the help of others, convinced an insurance company to cover her group. This was considered a real breakthrough, and the NRTA began to receive thousands of letters from retired people who *weren't* teachers but who wanted in on the insurance. And that's why the NRTA evolved into the AARP.

Today the AARP's goal is to improve every aspect of life for older people. With its enormous membership muscle, the group does this through legislative lobbying, research, and education. Besides offering its members several forms of insurance, the AARP runs a mail-order pharmacy that fills millions of prescriptions per year and publishes *AARP: The Magazine*, which, with its 22 million subscribers, has the world's largest magazine circulation.

Girls are more flexible and limber than boys.

Thanks to estrogen, the female hormone, our joints and muscles are looser, and thanks to our greater production of a hormone called relaxin, our ligaments, which tie muscles to bones, are softer and stretchier. For these reasons, we are more flexible than males, an advantage that prompted Long Island surgeon Elizabeth Coryllos to once remark in *Ms.* magazine, "The female is essentially a thoroughbred; the male is a quarter horse."

We retain this edge throughout life. A widely quoted statistic: at age sixty, women have 90 percent of both the strength and flexibility they had at age twenty; sixty-year-old men have only 60 percent.

Social biologist K. F. Dyer of the University of Adelaide in Australia wrote in his book *Challenging the Men: The Social Biology of Female Sporting Achievement* that our greater flexibility gives us "longer running strides, better hurdling techniques, and better kick and arm movements in swimming than would be expected on simple comparisons with men of the same height and weight."

The friendships between girls and women are richer, deeper, stronger, more intimate, and more affectionate than those between guys.

Researchers have confirmed that this is true—beginning in childhood and continuing through adolescence and into adulthood—in study after study. As a male writer once lamented in a *Newsweek* essay, "In our society, it seems as if you've got to have a bosom to be a buddy." What accounts for our higher-quality friendships? One reason, according to Letty Cottin Pogrebin, author of the book *Among Friends: Who We Like, Why We Like Them, and What We Do with Them*, is that in most cultures females are much more free to touch other females than males are to touch other males. And since touching—such as giving a hug—is the primary way to show affection, males don't show much affection to their male friends. (And, hey, most guys *need* a hug. Go to it, girls!)

Second, in conversation with their friends, females talk about much more intimate subjects than guys do with their guy friends, and this shared intimacy promotes closeness. According to Pogrebin, women communicate with their best friends on three levels: topical (politics, work, events), relational (the friendship itself), and personal (one's thoughts and feelings). Men, on the other hand, stick to topical subjects.

Why? Because men do not want to reveal their weaknesses to other men. "Men are supposed to be functional, to spend their time working or otherwise solving or thinking how to solve problems," wrote attorney Marc Feigen Fasteau, author of *The Male Machine*. "Personal reaction, how one feels about something, is considered dysfunctional, at best an irrelevant distraction from the expected objectivity." Dr. Myriam Miedzian, who has studied and written a lot about male behavior, puts it more simply and bluntly: "In the United States, adherence to the values of the masculine mystique makes intimate, self-revealing, deep friendships between men unusual." When psychotherapist Lillian B. Rubin, who wrote the book *Just Friends: The Role of Friendship in Our Lives*, did a study on the differences between male and female friendships, one of her male participants explained this inability to show vulnerability by saying, "I think men are afraid of each other. It's like we've been trained to be on guard."

On guard and *competitive*, according to Fasteau. Competitiveness is the principal way men relate to each other, he says, first because they don't know how else to make contact, and second because competitiveness is the perfect way to exhibit those key masculine traits like toughness and the ability to dominate. But this competitiveness, Fasteau says, is a barrier to openness between men.

Rubin says that when men have personal problems, they *will* attempt to discuss them with their guy friends, but what usually happens is "an abstract discussion, held under cover of an intellectual search for understanding rather than a revelation" of their lives and feelings. If a guy is worried about the constant fights he's having with his girlfriend, for example, he's more likely to launch a discussion of, say, the difficulty of communicating with women in general than to get specific about his own situation. Fasteau agrees: "Everything is discussed as though it were taking place out there somewhere, as though we had no more felt response to it than to the weather."

Another difference between female and male friendships: Both Pogrebin and Rubin say females *nurture* their friends and provide support, but males don't. Say, for example, a girl has a crisis, such as breaking up with a boyfriend. Here's how relationship expert Dr. Hu Fleming puts it: "[T]here appears to be a sound, heard only by the female population, when a fellow female is hurting from a breakup. They all flock together, one bringing the Häagen-Dazs, another with the old copy of *When Harry Met Sally*, and still another with the tickets to the latest Hot Male Review. Other women absolutely live for the opportunity to help their female compatriots through this tough time. Why? They've all been there, time and time again." Most guys don't do this for their guy friends because they consider nurturing to be *female* behavior.

Finally, the friendships of females are deeper and more meaningful than those of males because they are what Pogrebin calls more holistic. That is, female friends tend to do everything together, whereas guys tend to have different friends for different activities. For example, a man might have one friend to jog with, another for discussing work concerns, and a third for attending sports events. The roles of these friends rarely overlap. A girl, on the other hand, most likely does all of these things with the same person or persons.

What do guys lose because of these restrictions on their friendships? "The experience of knowing another person fully and completely and of *being* known himself," concludes Pogrebin. And what do women gain? Say Caryl Rivers, Rosalind Barnett, and Grace Baruch, who wrote the book *Beyond Sugar and Spice: How Women Grow, Learn, and Thrive*: "The friendships and the capacity for intimacy that girls develop while growing up may serve them in later years as a bulwark against loneliness, failure, and feelings of alienation. And these resources may be one of the great contributions of female socialization. Women in later life often find that this capacity for intimacy, which may have begun in the games of childhood, is a sustaining, life-giving force."

Women ushered in the nuclear age.

In Paris in the waning years of the nineteenth century, scientist Marie Curie coined the term *radioactivity* for the rays of energy that were spontaneously emitted from the elements uranium and thorium. She and her husband, Pierre, then went on to discover two new elements that were also radioactive—polonium, which Marie named after her native Poland, and radium, which they found to be two million times more radioactive than uranium. This work earned them a Nobel Prize in physics in 1903; Marie went on to win another Nobel Prize in chemistry in 1911 for isolating radium in its pure state (making her, for many decades, the only person ever to win two Nobel Prizes—and what makes that even more spectacular is that she got them in different disciplines).

Since then, radium has become an almost miraculous weapon against cancer, and Curie's discovery of the element is what she is actually noted for in the history books. But according to Rosalynd Pflaum, author of a Madame Curie biography called *Grand Obsession*, she made an even more important contribution: Madame Curie was the first to hypothesize that the atoms of radioactive material might yield immense energy . . . and that was the start of the nuclear age.

Marie's daughter, Irène Joliot-Curie, carried on her mother's work and in 1935 won her own Nobel in chemistry in conjunction with her husband, Frédéric Joliot-Curie. They had discovered that it's possible to make certain nonradioactive elements—like aluminum and magnesium—artificially radioactive. This was not only a vital step toward releasing the energy of the atom but also, like Marie's discovery, had immense therapeutic value. Today injections of Irène and Frédéric's artificially created radioisotopes, as they're called, are frequently used to treat leukemia.

Another scientist working in the field pioneered by Marie Curie, German physicist Lise Meitner, was the first to split the nucleus of a uranium atom (an atom being a basic part of a molecule, which is, in turn, a basic building block of all matter). She called this splitting of an atom nuclear fission.

Meitner, who first became interested in atomic physics when as a student she read newspaper stories about the Curie discovery of radium, was also the first scientist to calculate and report just how much energy potential nuclear fission had.

Later she would say that "we were unaware what kind of powerful genie we were releasing from a bottle." This was because, unfortunately, she made her discovery on the eve of World War II, and scientists in several countries immediately sought to turn this new source of energy into a weapon—a turn of events that Meitner adamantly opposed. Though she was invited to join the scientists who were at work on the weapon, she refused (in fact, the horrified Meitner stopped working on nuclear fission *period*). "I myself have not worked on smashing the atom with the idea of producing death-dealing weapons," she said. "You must not blame us scientists for the use to which war technicians put our discoveries." What those war technicians built was the atomic bomb that very nearly annihilated the entire Japanese city of Hiroshima in 1945.

Meitner's discovery, however, was life *saving* as well. It was essential to the continuing development of nuclear medicine, which the Curies' work had begun. And it is thanks to Meitner—whom Albert Einstein once called "the German Marie Curie"—that in these days of energy consciousness, dwindling natural resources, and high gas prices, we now have a new source of energy.

BONUS! **Females snore less than males.**

About one in four adults snore, but more of those snorers are men than women. Incidentally, researchers have measured snores as loud as 69 decibels, which is roughly as earsplitting as standing 10 feet from a jackhammer.

z z z z z z z z z

Girls have superior fine motor skills and manual dexterity.

In a laboratory setting, our more precise hand movements make us better than males—even when we're as young as three and a half—at tests like moving a row of small pegs from one area to another on a pegboard. Outside the laboratory—in real life—our dexterity makes us better at needlework and neurosurgery. And it gives us better handwriting. The explanation: Our muscles are controlled by two systems—the extra-pyramidal system, which controls all of our large muscles, and the pyramidal, which is in charge of fine movements. The female pyramidal system is better developed than the male. The female hormone estrogen probably plays a role in this, too, according to anthropologist Helen Fisher. She says our dexterity actually gets even better around ovulation, when our estrogen levels are at their highest.

Women made many of the biggest medical and scientific breakthroughs in the twentieth century and beyond.

We could go on for pages and pages about this, but let's not get bogged down with too much technical stuff, shall we? Don't want to lose any readers by using a whole bunch of Latin terms that have a thousand letters each.

Millions of people throughout the world have been saved thanks to the medical advances made by women. Among the many advances:

Pathologist Anna Wessel Williams developed a potent antitoxin for diphtheria during the early twentieth century when a raging diphtheria epidemic was underway. The disease was a major killer of children. Today diphtheria is rare in developed nations.

Also near the turn of the century, physician Dorothy Reed Mendenhall identified the cell that causes Hodgkin's disease, a form of cancer. Her discovery disproved the prevailing theory that Hodgkin's was a form of tuberculosis, a lung disease caused by a specific bacteria.

Edith Quimby, a biophysicist, gets the historical credit for developing the field of radiation therapy—that is, using X-rays and radium to treat cancer and other diseases in humans. Quimby did decades of research, beginning in 1919, to make it possible to determine the exact forms and dosages of radiation required for treatment.

In the first three decades of the twentieth century, toxicologist Alice Hamilton founded the discipline of industrial medicine and became the recognized authority in the field. The lives of thousands of workers were saved because Hamilton identified and sounded the alarm about toxic substances like lead, phosphorus, and benzol, which were then common in the air of factories, mines, and other workplaces. She crusaded for protective health legislation in regard to occupational diseases.

In 1930 the director of the esteemed Rockefeller Institute of Medical Studies in New York City called his employee anatomist Florence Sabin "the greatest living scientist." Among her many achievements: She was a pioneer in the study of blood, having discovered in 1919 the origin of red blood cells, which transport oxygen and carbon dioxide to and from the body tissues. Sabin was also the first to trace the origin and development of the lymphatic system—one of the body's most vital networks because it carries food to every single cell.

Bacteriologist Alice Evans found the source of a terrible disease called undulant fever, which was once very common throughout the world. The disease came from microorganisms living in the udders of healthy-looking cows. Then Evans came up with the solution to the problem: Pasteurize all milk; that is, heat it to kill the microorganisms before shipping it out to the market. Because of her, pasteurization of milk was mandated throughout the United States in the 1930s.

During that same decade, Hattie Alexander, a physician and bacteriologist, developed an antibody for *hemophilus influenzae* meningitis, a disease in which the membranes around the brain and spinal cord are inflamed. Within two years of Alexander's discovery, deaths from this type of meningitis, which had previously been 100 percent fatal in babies, fell by 80 percent.

Another major breakthrough in pediatric medicine in the 1930s was pathologist Ruth Darrow's research that showed how a mother with an RH-negative blood factor carrying an RH-positive fetus can develop antibodies that attack and destroy the fetus's red blood cells, ultimately killing the fetus. If you are RH-negative, you lack a protein that most people have on the surface of their red blood cells. Because of Darrow's research, all RH-negative mothers are now immunized against this process.

Other medical milestones from the 1930s: Pathologist and pediatrician Dorothy Hansine Andersen identified cystic fibrosis, then came up with an easy way to diagnose it. Nutritionist and biochemist Gladys Anderson Emerson, working with fellow scientist Herbert M. Evans, was the first to isolate vitamin E from wheat germ—a rich source of this vitamin, which today's researchers believe is a potent weapon against both cancer and heart disease. In England, Mary Walker discovered a cure for myasthenia gravis, a disease in which the voluntary muscles feel unusually fatigued. When Walker died in 1974, her obituary in a medical journal noted that hers was "the most important British contribution to therapeutic medicine up to that time."

Pediatrician Helen Taussig was responsible for developing the operation that saves "blue babies," whose skin appears bluish because of a shortage of oxygen in the blood. This condition was a lead cause of infant death before Taussig began researching it in the 1940s.

WHY IT'S GREAT TO BE A GIRL

In 1948 microbiologist Elizabeth Hazen and chemist Rachel Brown discovered nystatin, the first safe antiobiotic to kill fungi (fun guy!). Since then it's been used to cure everything from ringworm and athlete's foot to fungus growing on priceless art objects. Nystatin was considered the greatest biomedical breakthrough since penicillin had been discovered in 1928. Nystatin is to fungi what penicillin is to bacteria.

In 1952 when polio was the most dreaded disease in America, Dorothy Horstmann, a physician and research scientist at Yale, made a key discovery: Contrary to then-current belief, the polio virus did enter the bloodstream, not just the muscles. This information was vital to the development of the vaccine for polio, a disease causing muscle weakness and often paralysis.

Biologist Katherine Sanford gets the credit for cloning. She was the first person, in other words, to isolate a single cell and allow it to breed identical descendants. Besides providing a rich source of plot ideas for sci-fi writers, cloning makes possible the culturing of viruses, the development of vaccines, and the study of metabolic disorders.

Chemist Dorothy Mary Crowfoot Hodgkin won the Nobel Prize for chemistry in 1964 for her work in the 1940s and 1950s in determining the structure of certain chemical compounds by a technique called X-ray diffraction. She is especially known for deciphering the structure of penicillin, which was a big help in synthesizing and producing the huge quantities needed during World War II; the structure of vitamin B_{12}, important in the understanding and control of anemia (iron-poor blood); and the structure of insulin, which aided scientists in understanding diabetes.

Italian neurobiologist Rita Levi-Montalcini was a codiscoverer in 1954 of a biological mechanism called nerve growth factor, which stimulates the growth of nerve cells. This discovery played a vital role in helping researchers understand the way nerves act and function, and Levi-Montalcini won a Nobel in 1986 because of it. Today researchers around the world continue to study nerve growth factor because they believe it can help explain the nature of cancer, Alzheimer's, and other maladies.

A fourth Nobel Prize winner: Research scientist and pharmacology educator Gertrude Belle Elion. Back in the 1940s, Elion and her partner George Hitchings figured out how normal human cell growth differs from the growth of cancer, viruses, bacteria, and parasites. With that knowledge, Elion and Hitchings went on to develop drugs to fight cancer, herpes, gout, and other diseases, and to prevent organ rejection in kidney-transplant patients. They won the Nobel Prize in medicine in 1988 for their work.

Another trailblazer in the field of organ transplants was zoologist Barbara Bain, who developed a technique called mixed leukocyte culture (MLC) in the early 1960s. MLC plays a crucial role in organ and bone-marrow transplants by determining donor-recipient matches.

It's also thanks to a woman that the first drug to prolong the lives of people with AIDS came about. Although azidothymidine, commonly known as AZT, had been around since 1964—it was first synthesized as a potential cancer fighter and found ineffective for that purpose—it was chemist Janet Rideout who decided in the mid-1980s that it should be tested against HIV, the virus believed to cause AIDS. Another woman, virologist Martha St. Clair, performed the test, and when she checked her microscopic slide before leaving work one day, she found that the compound actually was inhibiting the growth of HIV. Said St. Clair in the book *Feminine Ingenuity* (1984): "It was a moment every researcher savors!"

In 1967 Jocelyn Bell Burnell, then a graduate student at England's Cambridge University, discovered the existence of pulsating stars, or pulsars. These are stars that emit radio signals. She wanted to keep this discovery a secret till she had done more research. But somehow word leaked out. And—whoa!—did that cause a furor among scientists and the general public. IT HAD TO MEAN THAT THERE REALLY ARE EXTRATERRESTIALS! Bell Burnell became a celebrity, but with all the attention being paid to her discovery, she was having a hard time getting her other work done. She began to complain about "little green men getting in the way." She even named the first pulsar she found LGM-1, for Little Green Men 1. Eventually scientists would conclude that the radio signals were a natural phenomenon and were not being sent by E.T.s. Pulsars are spinning stars or imploding stars. The professor that Bell Burnell was working under, Antony Hewish, won the 1974 Nobel Prize in physics for "his" discovery. It should come as no surprise that this ticked off a lot of people.

Ophthalmologist Patricia Era Bath was the first African American woman doctor to receive a patent for a medical invention. She received the patent in 1988 for an "Apparatus for ablating and removing cataract lenses," a version of a device designed to remove cataracts with a laser. A cataract is a clouding of the eye's natural lens, and it is a common problem among older people. Before Bath's invention, surgeons had to cut off cataracts with a metal blade <shudder>. Some of them still do.

Andrea Stierle, then a postdoctoral fellow at Montana State University, found in 1991 that a fungus growing on a yew tree—like the tree itself—contained taxol, a seemingly miraculous substance that in one study was found to significantly reduce tumors in 30 percent of women whose ovarian cancer did not respond to other treatments. Today, tamoxifen, as it is known, is also prescribed for breast and lung cancer.

German biologist and geneticist Christiane Nüsslein-Volhard and two American researchers, Edward B. Lewis and Eric F. Wieschaus, won the 2004 Nobel Prize in physiology or medicine for their trailblazing research into the genetic blueprint that turns a single cell into a fruit fly. The Nobel Prize Committee gave them the honor "for their discoveries concerning the genetic control of early embryonic development." In other words, their research may help to explain birth defects and miscarriages in humans.

Chocolate chip cookies baking in the oven, the oddly pleasant and nostalgic smells of Play-Doh, and a new box of Crayola crayons—these are but among a few of the ten thousand or more distinct odors our noses can identify. Microbiologist and immunologist Linda B. Buck has passionately studied exactly how we can detect odor molecules in the environment. Her research is considered groundbreaking and has provided important insight into the mechanism underlying our sense of smell. (BTW, if you haven't already read it, read #9.) And it is for this work that she and fellow American researcher Richard Axel won the 2004 Nobel Prize in physiology or medicine.

BONUS! Females get the hiccups only one-quarter as often as males do.

No one knows why this is so. Nor does anyone know why we get hiccups in the first place, since they serve no useful purpose. They don't protect the windpipe from inhaling food, as the gag reflex does. They don't clear the respiratory tract, as a sneeze does. They're just annoying, embarrassing, and sometimes even painful. (Our favorite cure for hiccups: swallowing a dry teaspoonful of white sugar. We don't know why this works, but trust us, it works better than anything else.)

37

Females aren't as sensitive to cold weather. And, ironically, we also stay cooler in the summer.

We have an extra layer of fat. It's just under the skin and it's thin, but it gives us seven more pounds of fat than males have. One researcher calls it an "invisible fur coat" for us in the winter. The extra fat layer also insulates us against the heat of summer. Our relative summer comfort can also be credited to the fact that our sweat glands are much more evenly distributed over our bodies than men's are, which allows us to cool off faster.

Females have a better sense of taste.

More sensitive, more discerning. Which explains why, in the past decade or so, women have expanded their opportunities to cook in kitchens other than our own (watch any cable food channel). While historically, master chefs have been men, in the future, more if not most of the world's greatest chefs will be women.

That we have more taste only stands to reason, since we have a superior sense of smell (see #9), and these "sister senses," as they're sometimes called, are linked. When we put food in our mouths, it stimulates the taste buds on our tongues, and small particles float into the nasal cavity to stimulate the organs of smell. The brain registers all of these nerve impulses from nose and mouth as a single sensation. This is why if your nose is stuffed up and you can't smell something, you can't taste it very well either.

The advantages of superior tasting ability? Besides makes eating more pleasurable, our heightened sense of taste makes us better at detecting whether or not a food might be spoiled or poisonous. Scientists speculate that evolution awarded us with great taste—our fourth superior sense (along with touch, hearing, and smell) among the five senses—because heightened senses were once essential for protecting and nurturing infants. There seems to be an estrogen link, since when levels of that hormone plummet after menopause (when our periods stop for the rest of our lives), many women report a decline in taste sensitivity. When England's Queen Victoria (see #10) was fifty-seven, for example, she complained that strawberries didn't taste as sweet as they had when she was a little girl.

The tasting ability of both women and men declines as we age for another reason—we lose taste buds. Throughout our lives, taste buds wear out, die, and are replaced within about a two-week span. But they're not replaced as frequently once we hit forty-five. A baby has far, far more taste buds than an adult (the kid even has some on the insides of her cheeks!), which may explain why most children don't count broccoli among their favorite foods.

We don't have to shave our faces.

Men aren't forced to either—but most of them feel obligated to shave for a clean-cut look. That commitment uses up an incredible 139 days (or 3,350 hours) of a man's lifetime. Those statistics, supplied by the Gillette Company, are based on the average man who's between fifteen and seventy-five years old and who shaves about three minutes a day five days a week.

Female faces haven't always been so razor-free, by the way. In the fourteenth and fifteenth centuries—as a look at Leonardo da Vinci's *Mona Lisa* will attest—women weren't considered fashionable unless they shaved off both their eyebrows plus an inch or two of hairline, resulting in a decidedly egghead effect. Later, in the sixteenth and seventeenth centuries, a permanently "surprised" look was all the rage, and since most women didn't have the eyebrows to carry it off, they shaved off their real ones and substituted false ones, often made of mouse fur.

Yes, the case can be made that many of us shave our legs and under our arms, but at least we can hide that hair if we are a few days late or don't shave in those places at all. Actually, most women in the world do *not* shave their legs or armpits. It is primarily the custom only in the United States and Great Britain and a few other Western countries. Shaving one's armpits didn't become fashionable in the United States till about 1917 and shaving one's legs till the early 1940s. There is no hygienic need to do either. The fashion magazines (and some advertisers) simply dictated that that would be the style. If you have any doubt of the power of fashion magazines, rent the DVD or read *The Devil Wears Prada.*

While we're on the subject of hair . . .

Women rarely go bald.

It's ironic that while males deal daily with hair where they don't want it, they usually have less hair where they *do* want it—on their heads. Both males and females shed about one hundred hairs a day. But while most of ours grow back, many guys lose those hairs permanently, thanks to the activity of the "male" hormone testosterone and a common inherited nuisance called male pattern baldness. A whopping 60 percent of all adult men in America are partially or completely bald. Yes, women *can* go bald, but that's rare, and it's usually the result of a disorder of the hair follicles, not heredity.

Incidentally, another advantage we have in the hair department is that our hair grows faster than that of males. So we recover more quickly from a bad haircut. Female hair grows faster at every age and fastest of all—up to seven inches in a single year—when we're between the ages of sixteen and twenty-four.

Women are responsible for the two biggest advances in computer programming ... and may also have invented the Internet!

Augusta Ada Byron, Countess of Lovelace is actually given credit for *inventing* computer programming. Programming is instructing the computer in its tasks. The Countess of Lovelace, daughter of the famous English poet Lord Byron (of "She walks in beauty" fame), was a recognized mathematical genius in her time, the mid-1800s. She became an associate of inventor George Babbage, who had already designed on paper a machine called the analytic engine, which could do complex calculations and is considered the forerunner of the digital computer. But it was she who devised the punch-card programs that would tell the analytic engine what to do. In 1982 the U.S. Department of Defense named a Pentagon computer language ADA in honor of Lady Lovelace's nineteenth-century contribution to science.

Rear Admiral Dr. Grace Murray Hopper (a woman of many talents) was the other female computer programming pioneer. In the early 1950s Hopper, who had a Ph.D. in mathematics from Yale and who'd had a hand in the development of the world's first electronic computer (the Navy's Mark I), invented the first computer "compiler." This was a translation program that allowed for the first automatic programming. It streamlined computer programming and changed software design forever by making the computer do a number of required, repetitive, tedious tasks automatically. Before Hopper's discovery, programmers were forced to write time-consuming instructions called codes every time they developed a new program, and they needed to have the equivalent of a Ph.D. in math to do it. The compiler is considered the ancestor to the computer language we now know as COBAL.

Hopper's compiler and some of her later work paved the way for what we today call user-friendly computer programs: programs that don't require that you know a complex computer code to operate a computer. For example, if you were to write a term paper about Grace Hopper on your computer and find, to your dismay, that you had misspelled the name as "Hoppre" throughout, to correct the mistake you need only give the computer a simple command like "Find Hoppre" instead of what was necessary in the olden days, something like [`#//-.##-+//**-{++}<<aee#//`2].

"Women turn out to be very good programmers for one very good reason," Hopper said in the book *Particular Passions*. "They tend to finish up things, and men don't very often finish. After men think they've solved a problem, they want to go off and get a new one, whereas a woman will always wrap it up in a neat package and document it."

In 1969 Hopper won the first-ever "Computer Science Man-of-the-Year Award" (tee-hee!) from the Data Processing Management Association (now the Association of Information Technology Professionals). And when Hopper finally retired from the Navy in

1986 as a rear admiral, she was eighty years old, the oldest officer on active duty in the entire U.S. military. In 1991 President George Herbert Walker Bush awarded her the U.S. Medal of Technology. She was the first individual ever, man or woman, to receive that honor. She died in 1992.

And last but certainly not least, we have Radia Perlman. In the mid-1970s she proposed a solution for routing information to vendors—that is, people or companies who were selling stuff to the company she then worked for, which taught children computer programming. She was largely ignored, mainly because she was female, but she wouldn't take no for an answer.

"Though she frequently found her audiences dismissive over the years," Peter Barlas wrote in a 2006 article on investors.com, "Perlman's spanning tree algorithm, which helps direct network traffic, became so embedded in the Internet's structure that she has been dubbed 'Mother of the Internet.' Any time a user searches through an engine such as Google, Perlman's algorithm forms a sort of road map to navigate the Internet."

Now we know why Al Gore, U.S. vice president under Bill Clinton, claimed he invented the Internet and has been rather viciously made fun of for that claim ever since. *He was just kidding!* Algor-ithm.

Anyway . . . Greg Papadopoulos, the Chief Technical Officer at Sun Microsystems, where Perlman is now a distinguished engineer, was quoted in Barlas's article as saying: "What Radia did was to put the basic traffic rules into place so it was possible to drive from one point to another without getting lost or driving in circles."

Girls are better at communicating their thoughts when instant messaging.

A recent study conducted by American University's Naomi Baron found, among other things, that when divided along gender lines, the messages between girls were more formal—with fewer contractions and better punctuation—than those between guys.

"The female IM looks more like a written genre, while the male IM looks more like a spoken genre," Baron told *LifeScience* in an interview.

Women will eventually outperform men in several of the most strenuous sports.

Until the early 1970s no one disputed that men were superior at most sports. But once women began to get coaching and training that had been traditionally available only to men, our performance levels in such strenuous sports as swimming and running jumped suddenly and much more sharply than those of men. Example: Between 1963 and 1978 the best female marathon time fell from 3:50 hours to 2:50 hours, whereas the male time went from 2:20 to 2:10.

In the early 1990s researchers applying these rates of improvement predicted that women would overtake men in marathon running within the 1990s (didn't happen/hasn't happened yet), in cycling by the year 2011 (could happen), and in speed swimming by 2056.

This is cool: Physicist Randall Woods of the British Columbia Institute of Technology has predicted that in 2271, women marathon runners will not only surpass men in speed but will run faster than the fastest land animal on earth—the cheetah.

Women surpassed men in swimming the chilly English Channel in 1926 when Gertrude Ederle became the first woman to swim the channel. Her time broke the record of the fastest male channel swimmer by a whopping two hours. While a man, Christof Wandratsch, broke the latest speed record in 2005, England's Alison Streeter holds the Channel Swimming Association's title of Queen of the Channel, having made forty-three crossings, more than anyone in the world.

Another amazing long-distance open-water swimmer is American Lynne Cox. She was the first to cross the Catalina Island Channel in California in 1971. She has twice held the record for the fastest crossing of the English Channel, in 1972 and 1973. In 1976 Cox was also the first person to swim Chile's Straits of Magellan; the first to cross the Skagerrak, a strait that runs between Norway and Denmark (brr!); and the first to swim around the Cape of Good Hope in South Africa, where she risked running into sharks, jellyfish, and sea snakes.

Cox is best known for being the first person, in 1987, to swim across the Bering Strait between Alaska and what was then the Soviet Union. The water temperature was a brisk (!) 40 degrees. This accomplishment actually eased Cold War—a decades-long standoff between the Communist Soviet Union and the Democratic countries—tensions because then President Ronald Reagan and Soviet head Mikhail Gorbachev met in Washington, D.C., to jointly congratulate her on her success. Many people think that Cox's most remarkable feat was swimming more than a mile in the freezing waters of Antarctica (brrr! x 1,000). In most humans, hypothermia—a condition in which the core body temperature drops below normal, a condition that can be damaging and even fatal—would set in within five minutes. Cox was in the water for twenty-five minutes.

Our extra fat, which better insulates us against cold water (see #37), is one reason females are superior in long-distance open-water swimming. But we make better swimmers than guys *period*. Our greater flexibility (see #32) is a big help here. And the greater amount of fat in our bodies provides us with better buoyancy and less drag, with the result that we use 20 percent less energy than men do when we swim. The higher level of fat in our thighs, especially, makes it easier for us to hold our legs horizontal in the water, a position necessary for the most efficient leg action. It has even been suggested that our breasts may also be an advantage in swimming by aiding the passage of water over the body.

Girls are luckier in love.

43

For one thing, girls and women experience the joy of being in love more intensely than boys and men do. When in love, we are more likely to report feeling "giddy and carefree," "like I'm floating on a cloud," and "like I want to run, jump, and scream." We report higher levels of euphoria than guys and more of a general feeling of well-being. T. George Harris (founder of *Psychology Today* magazine) said in social psychologist Elaine Hatfield and G. William Walster's book *A New Look at Love* (2002): "Women's bodies are kinder to them, more generous, because in passionate love they feel more physical highs." (Though he added that this euphoria also causes us to lose more sleep when we're in love than men do!)

Women are also at an advantage when we fall *out* of love: We get over the breakup of a relationship more easily than guys do. Charles T. Hill, professor of psychology at Whittier College, said in Anne Campbell's book *The Opposite Sex*: "Rejected men have more difficulty coping emotionally with the breakup than women in the same situation. Men become more depressed and lonely, and they have a harder time remaining friends with their former partner after the breakup." Backing him up is a study by Harvard scientists of the relationships of twenty-one Boston couples. These researchers, who followed the relationships for two years, concluded that women were far more resigned at the end of a relationship and were therefore better able to "pick up the pieces" and move on. Interestingly, and contrary to popular belief, the researchers also found that it was usually the women who decided whether and when a relationship should end.

Why is breaking up so hard on men? An article in *Cosmopolitan* magazine came up with several reasons; we'll review just a few. According to New York City family therapist Vera Paster, most men don't monitor the quality of a relationship the way most women do. So when a woman breaks it off, it comes as a big shock to the average guy. Unlike women, men tend to seal up their pain instead of dealing with it, and it's the crying, talking to friends, and working through that women do that's the true source of healing, says Paster (See Dr. Hu Fleming's comment in #33. It also doesn't help here that guys have more difficulty expressing their emotions [see #5] in the first place.)

And according to *Cosmo*, although the stereotype of the male is that he is more independent than the female, males seem to have a special susceptibility to separation and loss. As toddlers, boys have to abandon their fantasies to be just like Mommy, and around the time they start kindergarten they have to come to grips with the reality that they can't marry her. "Although part of normal development," according to *Cosmo*, "these losses can be traumatic. They lead psychologists like [Sam] Osherson to suspect that vulnerability to separation and loss is virtually built in to the male condition."

Women founded and/or head up some of the world's largest, oldest, and unique companies in the world.

* Early film star Mary Pickford cofounded United Artists Corporation, a filmmaking studio, with three other actors in 1919. It's still around today, producing such memorable movies as *The Bird Cage* (1996), *Hotel Rwanda* (2004), and *Capote* (2005).

* Laura Scudder was a California entrepreneur who made and sold potato chips and pioneered the packing of potato chips in sealed bags. Before Scudder founded her company in 1926, potato chips were packed in tins or barrels. The problem: That kind of packaging left chips at the bottom stale and crumbled. Scudder began having her employees take home sheets of wax paper to iron into bags. These were filled with the potato chips the next day. This creative idea kept the chips fresh and crisp longer and, along with the invention of cellophane, enabled potato chips to become mass-marketed for the first time. Scudder, who became known as The Potato Chip Queen, was also the first to put freshness dates on products. She finally sold her company for $6 million in 1957, and Borden bought it thirty years later for $100 million. You can still find Laura Scudder brand chips, such as Laura Scudder's Salt and Pepper Classic Potato Chips. *Pepper?*

* Industrialist Olive Beech formed the Beech Aircraft Company with her husband, Walter, in the 1930s. In 1980 Beech Aircraft merged with the Raytheon Aircraft Company, which still has a Beechcraft line.

* Estée Lauder started a kitchen business in the 1930s blending face creams and built it into a multimillion-dollar international cosmetics empire. Besides the Estée Lauder brand, other product lines have included Clinique, Aramis, Prescriptives, and Origins. It was Lauder who came up with the concept of offering a free gift with the purchase of a cosmetic or cologne. In 1998 Lauder was the only woman on *Time* magazine's "Twenty Most Influential Business Geniuses of the Century." Secret to her success: "I have never worked a day in my life without selling. If I believe in something, I sell it, and I sell it hard," she once said. She died at age ninety-seven. Her two sons are among the top 300 richest people in the world.

* In 1947 Eileen Ford founded Ford Models, an internationally known modeling agency that continues to thrive. "I live and breathe on the length of a skirt," she once said. "I'm crazy about fashion, that's all. My soul is devoted to it. I love to see changes in makeup and hair. Fashion changes all the time." Ain't that the truth.

* Dame Anita Roddick started The Body Shop in Brighton, England, in 1976. She has been called "a key pioneer of socially responsible business"—her company, for example, considers testing on animals "to be morally and scientifically indefensible," according to her Web site. Roddick's company sells high-quality skin and body care

products. There are more than 1,900 outlets in 50 countries spanning 25 languages and 12 time zones. She was named a Dame of the Order of the British Empire in 2003. That's the female version of being knighted by the queen. Knighted guys are called "Sir," such as "Sir Elton John."

❋ Debbi Fields, a young mother with no business experience, opened her first cookie store in Palo Alto, California, in 1977. Everybody told her she was nuts. No business could survive by just selling cookies (ha ha!). Those "humble beginnings launched Mrs. Fields into a worldwide celebrity and made her company the premier chain of cookie and baked goods stores," according to the company's Web site.

❋ Donna Karan cofounded Donna Karan International in 1984. She is a famous fashion designer and maven. She is nicknamed the Queen of Seventh Avenue (that's New York City's hub of the fashion business). "Everything I do is a matter of heart, body, and soul," she says on the company's Web site. She credits her feminine instincts (see #6) for the company's success. "Design is a constant challenge to balance comfort with luxe, the practical with the desirable," Karan says. The company now has myriad divisions—it sells not just clothes for women but men's wear, beauty products, and home furnishings.

❋ Oprah Winfrey founded HARPO (Oprah spelled backward) Productions in 1986. Her company has been called "a formidable force in film and television production." Besides her internationally successful talk show, her "influence extended to the publishing industry when she began an on-air book club," according to the Academy of Achievement (U.S.). "Oprah Book Club selections became instant bestsellers." She is also the founder and editorial director of *O: The Oprah Magazine*, which is published by the Hearst Corporation and has a 2.4 million circulation. Here's a great quote from Oprah, who had a pretty terrible childhood overall: "It doesn't matter who you are, where you came from. The ability to triumph begins with you. Always." For more about Oprah, see #45.

❋ Martha Stewart founded Martha Stewart Living Omnimedia— *Martha Stewart Living* magazine, books, television shows, a satellite radio program, products, etc. In 2005 the company had more than $232 million in sales. Going to prison obviously did not tarnish Stewart's image.

❋ Former supermodel Kathy Ireland is the founder (in 1993), chief executive officer, and chief designer of Kathy Ireland Worldwide. The primary mission of her company is "finding solutions for families, especially busy moms." *Forbes* magazine reports that her company is a "design empire which grosses over one billion dollars annually in retail sales." Kathy Ireland Worldwide sells flooring, rugs, coverings, bedding, mattresses, candles, apparel, and jewelry. So see? There is life after you cease to be a popular model.

❋ Janese Swanson, who grew up poor and who has six college degrees including a doctorate, founded Girl Tech in 1995. Before that, she had created the mega-hit "Where in the World Is Carmen San Diego?" for another software company. She founded Girl Tech because, in the early 1990s, she had become disturbed by the fact that, as usual, girls were being "left out" of technology. At Girl Tech, she created games, products, and services that encouraged girls ages eight to twelve to use new technologies, such as the Internet and video games. In 1998 she sold Girl Tech to Radica Games Limited. It continues to thrive to this day.

❋ Linda Torres-Winters founded Lindita's Instant Salsa Mixes in the 1990s. The daughter of migrant workers, she grew up picking tomatoes in the American Midwest. She picked her first tomatoes in the field at the age of six. "What she didn't know then was that it was tomatoes—stirred together with determination and seasoned with inspiration—that would lead to entrepreneurial success," according to the U.S. Small Business Administration. "I can remember my mother making the best salsa," she told the SBA. Starting with that inspiration, she created a salsa mix with a twist: It's dry, based on dehydrated spices and vegetables Torres-Winters used on family camping trips, says the SBA. "You just add fresh or canned tomatoes for 'homemade' salsa, any time, anywhere. What's more, you can either have it hot or mild." From her Web site: "The fresh tomatoes option tastes better than any other bottled salsa!" Her company's products are now available in five hundred stores (such as Safeway) in eight states.

❋ In 2000 Sue Wilson, Janet Rickstrew, and Mary Tatum, three close friends and do-it-yourselfers, founded Tomboy Tools. Their mission is to teach women to be confident and competent homeowners and do-it-yourselfers. They also sell tools especially designed for women. One of their mottos: "No pink tools!"

Here are the women who are the chief executive officers of *Fortune* magazine's list of the top 500 companies in the United States:

❋ Meg Whitman, eBay. She was on *Time* magazine's 2004 list of "The World's Most Influential People" because "Whitman is the quiet giant of the Internet World, one of a mere handful of Silicon Valley CEOs who survived the [collapse of] the dotcom bubble [around 2000] with her reputation unscathed."

❋ Indira K. Nooyi, PepsiCo. Nooyi was born and educated in India. Her company not only produces Pepsi products, but several other brands as well, including Fritos, Lays, Tropicana, Cracker Jack, Quaker Oats, and Rice-A-Roni.

❋ Andrea Jung, Avon Products. (Bet she gets a lot of free makeup!)

❋ Patricia Russo, Lucent Technologies. Supplier of high-tech solutions.

❋ Susan M. Ivey, Reynolds American. Cigarettes!

❋ Mary Sammons, Rite Aid. There are 3,323 Rite Aid drugstores in the United States.

❋ Anne Mulcahy, Xerox. No explanation needed.

And now, a few more interesting stories . . .

In the early 1900s Madame C. J. Walker created the first cosmetics and hair products designed specifically for African Americans. While she initially mixed up her concoctions in her laundry tub, by 1917 Walker's was the largest business in the United States owned by an African American. The *Guinness Book of World Records* cites Walker as the first female American self-made millionaire. She used her wealth to help promote and expand economic opportunities for others, particularly African Americans.

And then there was Ruth Handler, who cofounded Mattel in Los Angeles in 1945 with her husband, Elliot, and Harold "Matt" Matson. The name was a marriage of given names: Matt + El. "It never even occurred to me that some part of 'Ruth,' by all rights, belonged in the name," she wrote in her autobiography *Dream Doll: The Ruth Handler Story.* "But this was 1945, and just as a woman got her identity through her husband in her personal life—you were Mrs. John Smith, not Sally Smith—should it not be so in business?" Hmm . . . if they had founded that company, say, last year, it would be called Rumattel or something like that.

Mattel started as a garage business that made picture frames. The guys produced them and Ruth went out and sold them and made the deliveries. Soon, however, Elliot started a side business making dollhouse furniture from picture frame scraps, and Matson sold his share of the company to the Handlers (a decision he no doubt lived to regret!). The Handlers turned the company's focus to toys.

Elliot was a master toymaker, creating such legendary products as Hot Wheels and See 'n Say. Ruth was a marketing genius. She ran the business side of Mattel. But it was she who came up with the concept and the design of the Barbie doll. Ruth got the idea after she noticed that her daughter Barbara (nicknamed Barbie), who loved paper dolls, didn't want to play with baby or child figure paper dolls. She much preferred teenage or adult women paper dolls. She was fantasizing about how life would be when she grew up.

In the mid-1970s, after Ruth and Elliot were forced out of Mattel, Ruth spent a few miserable years deeply depressed. Then one day she came up with an idea. She would make the first really natural-looking breast prosthesis (fake breast) for women like her who had had a mastectomy for breast cancer. She called the company "Nearly Me" and was once again successful. For a while, the company's slogan was "The best manmade breast is made by a woman."

Ruth, who was criticized for decades because of the size of Barbie's boobs, told a reporter: "When I first conceived [the] Barbie [doll], I believed it was important to a little girl's self-esteem to play with a doll that has breasts. Now I find it even more important to return that self-esteem to women who had lost theirs."

When she began to have heart problems, she finally sold Nearly Me, in 1991, to Spenco Medical, a subsidiary of Kimberly Clark.

To sum this entry up, the bad news is that women run fewer than 2 percent of *Fortune* 500 companies. And that there is still a "glass ceiling"—the notion that women can rise up only to a certain level in a corporation. We can speak from personal experience. A relative of ours was the director of a department for a major corporation. When she finally left the job, she was replaced by a guy who was brought in as a vice-president—a better title with a higher salary.

The good news is that the number of woman-founded businesses continues to rise every year. According to the U.S. Census Bureau's 2002 Survey of Business Owners, the number of women-owned businesses grew 20 percent between 1997 and 2002, twice as much as the national average. There were 6.5 million woman-owned businesses in 2002, and they generated more than $940 *billion* in revenues. So you can always do what many of the above-mentioned women did: Find your niche. Come up with a product or service that people need or will want and *be your own boss.*

A woman is considered "the moral leader of the millennium."

T he Divine Miss O. Oprah Winfrey. She is *always* on *Time* magazine's annual list of the world's most influential people. An amazing number of people are now turning to her show for spiritual guidance. *The Oprah Winfrey Show* is watched by 49 million people a week in 122 countries, including countries where you would not expect it to be broadcast, such as Afghanistan, Iran, and Saudi Arabia. A poll taken by the religious Web site BeliefNet.com in November 2005 really raised eyebrows: "One out of three of the people polled said Oprah has had a more profound impact on their spiritual lives than even their priests, their rabbi, or their pastors," according to CNN culture and entertainment reporter and anchor Brooke Anderson, who is also a correspondent for CNN's *Showbiz Tonight*, which featured a segment on this subject in 2006. Some other comments made on that show:

Marcia Z. Nelson, author of *The Gospel According to Oprah* (2005): "[T]here's a religion that's about what we should believe, and then there's religion that emphasizes how we should act or how we should live. And Oprah is religious in the second sense. She's always been about how we should live."

New York Times reporter Lola Ogunnaike: "A lot of people are looking at Oprah as the new moral leader of the millennium. In this day and age, everyone's all about sensationalism and sex sells, and sex sells. I would argue that Oprah has found a way to make spirituality sexy."

Supermodel Tyra Banks: "She's our Mother Teresa. She really is. Except she's not working barefoot. She has on some stilettos to work it out."

Mariah Carey: "She is one of those people who has changed the world."

An unidentified male: "O, if you run for president, I'm voting."

Interestingly, Winfrey herself apparently disagrees with all of this idolization. When Barbara Walters asked her, on the American talk show *The View*, "You are now considered a guru?" Winfrey responded, "No, I'm not. I really am just doing the best I can. I feel like I'm a work in progress."

Back to *Show Biz Tonight* correspondent Brooke Anderson: "A woman in progress. A woman with a message of charity. . . . Oprah is not ordained. She doesn't preach in the traditional sense, and she doesn't go overboard on religion."

Oprah Winfrey: "I say give the people the roses while they live. Don't waste it on a casket."

Anderson: "Still, she spreads the word, a word of generosity, gratitude, and forgiveness."

Speaking of Winfrey's generosity, Forbes.com named Oprah one of the ten most generous celebrities in 2006. According to *Forbes* magazine, she gave $52 million to charity in 2005.

Women created some of television's most groundbreaking sitcoms.

Let's begin with *I Love Lucy*, which was cocreated by Lucille Ball and her husband, Desi Arnaz, in the 1950s. The CBS network had offered Ball a TV series based on a successful "husband and wife" radio series in which she had performed. She liked the idea but insisted that on TV, unlike in her radio series, her real-life husband would have the husband role. The network balked because Arnaz was a "foreigner" (he was from Cuba) and the higher-ups didn't think Americans would accept them as a couple. Nevertheless, Ball persisted and got her way. *I Love Lucy* was a smash hit from the very beginning, proving, among other things, that the public was okay with a non-"whitebread" marriage. *I Love Lucy* was also groundbreaking in that Lucy was not content to be a sweet, simple housewife, much to the annoyance of husband Ricky Ricardo. Lucy Ricardo wanted to be in show business just like her husband was, and many of the funniest episodes involved Ricky's attempts to keep Lucy off his nightclub stage.

Another—and major—first of this show, and this was largely thanks to Arnaz, was that it was filmed. That made it possible to have a high-quality print of each episode in comparison to the poor-quality "kinescope" method that ruled at the time. That is also why *I Love Lucy* will be in reruns until the day the world ends. In addition,

I Love Lucy pioneered the use of three cameras instead of just one, to allow for editing of the finished product. The appeal of reusable filmed programs grew, eventually resulting in the shift of television from New York, where the industry started, to Los Angeles, where the film facilities were. *I Love Lucy* was also the first series to be filmed in front of a live audience.

Next up, beginning in 1975, was *One Day at a Time*, about a mother who was simultaneously coping with a full-time job and raising two headstrong teenage girls. Cocreated by Whitney Blake and her husband, Allan Manings, what was groundbreaking about this show was that Ann Romano, the mom, was divorced. Up until that time, the very few shows with single female leads were either widows, such as Lucille Ball in *The Lucy Show* and *Here's Lucy*, or never married and childless, such as Marlo Thomas in *That Girl* and Mary Tyler Moore in *Mary Tyler Moore*. In the latter series, the original plan was to make Mary a divorcée, but the topic of divorce was still such a hot button in 1970, the year the show premiered, that the producers decided she would be a never-been-married. Some interesting factoids about *One Day at a Time*'s late cocreator Whitney Blake, who had been an actress herself: Singer/actress Whitney Houston was named after her, and she was the mother of Meredith Baxter (best known for her role as the mom in the 1980s sitcom *Family Ties*).

The Golden Girls, created by Susan Harris in the mid-1980s, was the first series to portray older women characters (four of them living together in a Miami house) as not just "older" but in great shape, relatively happy, and, most important, *normal*. In fact, very few of the shows dealt with aging. Most episodes involved issues all women deal with—such as problems with boyfriends and annoying relatives, fighting with the people you live with, and making mistakes. Furthermore, the show exploded stereotypes about women over fifty. Dorothy (played by Bea Arthur) had an incredibly stylish wardrobe, for example, and man-crazy Blanche (played by Rue McClanahan) was sexy. In one episode, Blanche's morality is tested when a male teacher in an adult education class hits on her and promises her a good grade in exchange for sex.

Roseanne, which began its nine-year run in 1988, was the first sitcom to depict a more typical white American family. *Roseanne* was about a lower-middle-class family struggling with money, marriage, children, and other everyday problems. While the series was created by a man, Matt Williams, comedian Roseanne Barr (who portrayed the lead character) had a heavy hand in the show's production and scripts (and eventually fired Williams). Most refreshingly, Roseanne was the first sitcom mom who acted like *a real mom*. Unlike June Cleaver of *Leave it to Beaver* and Carol Brady of *The Brady Bunch*, Roseanne yelled at her kids, was kind of messy, and said stuff like, "Get outta here. I'm busy." Speaking of Carol Brady, one of the greatest mysteries of our time is, since Carol didn't have a job and did little (if any) visible community or school volunteer work, what did she do all day and *why did she need Alice?* Another mystery for the ages: Since six kids had to share ONE bathroom, why didn't Mike Brady, an architect, *add on another bathroom?*

Girls have longer attention spans than boys.

Psychologist Diane McGuinness, Emeritus Professor of Psychology at the University of South Florida, conducted numerous studies of gender differences in preschool children. In one study she found that in a twenty-minute interval, girls started and *finished* more projects than boys. The boys were simply more distractible—they stopped their play to look at something else four times more often than girls. They also spent more time watching other kids.

Nature was kinder to females when it came to genital design. Yours are tucked safely inside, protected from cold and injury.

It's the perfect answer for your daughter if she asks, "Why don't I have a penis?"

Here's the way one mother explained it to her seven-year-old daughter: "You've ridden a boy's ten-speed bicycle, right? And surely at least once you've accidentally slid off the seat and landed hard on the bar that connects it with the handlebars. You know that agony? Well, multiply that by ten and you've got a rough idea of what it feels like to be a boy when he does that."

Here's Madonna on the subject: "I wouldn't want a penis. It would be like having a third leg. It would seem like a contraption that would get in the way."

And here's what the late and beloved Mister Rogers once said: "Boys are fancy on the outside, girls on the inside." Be profoundly glad of that!

We smile more than guys do, and people of both sexes smile more at us.

48

Numerous studies back this up, including a 1999 study at Valdosta State University in Georgia called "Gender Differences in Non-verbal Communication." That research also backed up other studies that girls and women are more attracted to others who smile.

So what is the value of a smile? The legendary motivational speaker and writer Dale Carnegie, who wrote *How to Win Friends and Influence People* (latest edition, 1990), said smiling helps you do just that. Other research backs this up and has shown that a smiling person is judged to be more sincere, competent, pleasant, sociable, and attractive than a non-smiling person. There is also some evidence that if you smile when you are caught doing something wrong, people will be more lenient with you!

BONUS!

As babies, girls are less fearful and irritable than boys, cry less often, smile more frequently, and are quicker to potty train.

The latter is because the nerve endings that provide the sensation to the brain that says "I've got to go!" develop later in boys than girls. Obviously, you won't be able to appreciate this kind of thing until you have your own baby girl!

It's thanks to women that so many American girls go on to become athletic superstars.

49

Title IX revolutionized school sports when it became law in 1972. It banned sex discrimination in programs and activities at any school that received federal grant money. In other words, if a high school spent X amount on boys' sports, they had to spend the same amount on girls' sports. Now come on, you don't think a *guy* would have fought for this, do you? Women did, led by U.S. Congress Representative Edith Green of Oregon, aided by the research done by Dr. Bernice Resnick Sander and with the support, among others, of fellow Representatives Patsy Takemoto Mink of Hawaii (the first woman of color in the U.S. Congress) and Shirley Chisholm of New York (the first African American Congresswoman).

Title IX was part of a larger bill that passed, the Education Bill of 1972, also spearheaded by Green, who had worked her way up to the House Education Committee to become chairwoman of one of its three subcommittees, the one that focused on higher education. The larger bill did a whole lot of other things besides giving girls and women greater opportunities to play sports. It also, for example, prohibited the gender quota system in colleges. Before the bill passed, it was very common for colleges to set a limit on the number of women it would accept—say, 30 percent of an incoming freshman class.

Green and her colleagues fought a tough battle. Some of the Congressmen called her "the wicked witch of the West" behind her back, and during one hearing a man sarcastically said something along the lines of "Next we'll be having male stewardesses!" (LOL).

Title IX's impact has been spectacular. According to the excellent book *Let Me Play: The Story of Title IX, the Law That Changed the Future of Girls in America* (2005), in 1971–1972 the total number of high school boys participating in varsity sports was 3,666,917; girls, 294,015. In 2001–2002, those numbers had changed to 3,960,517 boys and 2,806,998 girls. The gains are relatively similar for women participating in college sports.

Soccer superstar Mia Hamm (born in 1972) is only one example of how Title IX changed everything. One of the world's most popular athletes, she has scored more goals than any other female soccer player on earth. Hamm helped the United States win two World Cups and an Olympic gold medal. She has also inspired thousands of kids to play soccer.

As for Congresswoman Green, who died in 1987, according to *Let Me Play*: "When she looked back in her final years, Mrs. Green remained most proud of her efforts to expand educational opportunities for all and to create possibilities for girls and women, especially through Title IX. Her greatest satisfaction in her work had come in spending months or years on a law and watching it take effect."

Only women can give birth.

Babies have been *conceived* in a test tube, but so far no embryo has developed into a viable human being outside the body of a woman.

While we're on the subject of bearing children: Venerable anthropologist Margaret Mead once speculated that perhaps the reason that in the past there weren't more standout women in some of the creative fields, such as music composition, was "the greater appeal of creating and cherishing young human beings."

And maybe that *is* it, in combination with the fact that for centuries women were actively discouraged—if not outright prohibited—from doing anything outside the confines of bearing children and keeping house.

But it's a different world now. We are living in a time in which females can choose to raise children or to engage in creative, satisfying work outside the home, or to even do both—either at different times in our lives (remember, on average we've got an extra six years to play with) or, with lots of help, simultaneously. The choice is ours, and even the sky is no longer the limit (just ask Sally Ride). That's why now, more than at any other time in history, it's great to be a girl, wonderful to be a woman, fantastic to be female.

A Final Note from Jacqueline Shannon

I have devoted a large part of my writing life to helping girls and women with their self-confidence, mainly because I lost mine for so many years. In my early thirties, I discovered that these things are true:

❋ That if you hang in there long enough, it gets better.
❋ That outside of high school, it's an advantage to be different.
❋ That despite appearances, *nobody* has it all.

And here is something I learned since I wrote the first edition of this book:

❋ Once you've gone through your twenties, with every year you age, you care less and less about what people think about you. See? Aging has its beneits.

Carry on.

Suggested Reading List

GENERAL

America's Women: Four Hundred Years of Dolls, Drudges, Helpmates, and Heroines by Gail Collins. Harper Perennial, reprint edition, 2004.

Brain Sex: The Real Difference Between Men and Women by Ann Moir, Ph.D., and David Jessel. Delta, 1992.

Early Man in the New World by (historians) Kenneth MacGowan and Joseph A. Hester. Sage Publications, 1983.

The Female Brain by Louann Brizendine, M.D. Morgan Road Books, 2006.

The First Sex: The Natural Talents of Women and How They Are Changing the World by (anthropologist) Helen Fisher. Ballantine Books, 2002.

The Natural Superiority of Women, fifth edition, by Ashley Montagu (a man). AltaMira Press, 1999.

Especially for Young Readers

Cool Women: The Thinking Girl's Guide to the Hippest Women in History, edited by Pam Nelson. Girl Press, 2001. Ages 9 and up.

Girls Who Rocked the World: Heroines from Sacagawea to Sheryl Swopes by Amelie Welden. Beyond Words Publishing, 1998. Ages 9 to 13. This book covers girls/women who achieved "something extraordinary" before age twenty.

Girls Who Rocked the World 2: Heroines from Harriet Tubman to Mia Hamm by Michelle Roehm. Beyond Words Publishing, 2000. Ages 9 to 13. This is a follow-up book to the title above.

Web sites

Biographies of women who contributed to our culture in many different ways: www.distinguishedwomen.com.

Girls Can Do: Helping Girls Discover Their Life's Passions. Web site for girls ages 8 to 18: www.girlscando.com.

GO Girls Only! Girl Scouts of the U.S.A. Web site for girls ages 5 to 12: www .gogirlsonly.org.

Girl Power—Empowering Girls Worldwide. Australian site: www.girl.com.au.

Girls Inc.—Inspiring All Girls to Be Strong, Smart, and Bold: www.girlsinc.org.

GirlSite! Network: www.girlsite.org.

Girl Zone: Where Every Girl Is Cool: www.girlzone.com.

SmartGirl, a Web site for girls, by girls, where you can share your thoughts and ideas: www.smartgirl.org.

Studio 2B: The Place for Teens. Girl Scouts of the U.S.A. Web site: www.studio 2b.org.

SUSAN B. ANTHONY

Especially for Young Readers

Fighting for Equal Rights: A Story About Susan B. Anthony by Maryann N. Weidt. Lerner Publishing Group, 2003. Ages 8 to 10.

Susan B. Anthony: Fighter for Women's Rights by Deborah Hopkinson. Aladdin, 2005.

BABE DIDRIKSON

Especially for Young Readers

Babe Didrikson: The Greatest All-Sport Athlete of All Time by Susan E. Cayleff. Conari Press, 2000. Ages 9 to 12.

Babe Didrikson Zaharias by Russell Freedman. Clarion Books, 1999. Ages 10 and up.

ENVIRONMENT/ENVIRONMENTALISTS

Rachel Carson: Witness for Nature by Linda Lear. Owl Books, reprint edition, 1998.

Sea Change: A Message of the Oceans by Sylvia Earle. Ballantine Books, 1996.

Silent Spring by Rachel Carson. Mariner Books, Fortieth Anniversary edition, 2002.

Especially for Young Readers

Rachel Carson: Preserving a Sense of Wonder by Thomas Locker and Joseph Bruchac. Fulcrum Publishing, 2004.

Rachel: The Story of Rachel Carson by Amy Ehrlich. Silver Whistle, 2003. Ages 6 to 10.

Studio 2B Focus: Parks Matter, a Girl Scouts of the U.S.A. book, available at www.studio2b.org/boutique/.

Web site

Pioneer, environmentalist, catalyst, Pittsburgher: www.rachelcarson.org.

INVENTORS/INVENTIONS

Mothers of Invention: From the Bra to the Bomb, Forgotten Women and Their Unforgettable Ideas by Ethlie Ann Vare and Greg Ptacek. Quill, 1989. Out of print; check your library.

Patently Female: From AZT to TV Dinners, Stories of Women Inventors and Their Breakthrough Ideas by Ethlie Ann Vare and Greg Ptacek. Wiley, 2002. This is a sequel to their book *Mothers of Invention*.

Especially for Younger Readers

Brainstorm!: The Stories of Twenty American Kid Inventors by Tom Tucker. Farrar, Straus, and Giroux, 1998. Ages 10 to 14.

Girls & Young Women Inventing: Twenty True Stories About Inventors Plus How You Can Be One Yourself by Frances A. Karnes, Ph.D., and Suzanne M. Bean, Ph.D. Free Spirit Publishing, 1995. Ages 10 and up. Out of print; check your library.

Girls Think of Everything: Stories of Ingenious Inventions by Women by Catherine Thimmesh. Houghton Mifflin, 2000. Ages 10 and up.

The Kids' Invention Book by Arlene Erlbach. Lerner Publications, 1999. Ages 9 to 11.

So You Want to Be an Inventor? by Judith St. George. Philomel, 2002. Ages 4 to 8.

Web sites

Women inventors: http://inventors.about.com/od/womeninventors/.

LEADERS/LEADERSHIP

The Female Advantage: Women's Ways of Leadership by Sally Helgesen. Currency, 1995.

Madam President: Women Blazing the Leadership Trail by Eleanor Clift and Tom Brazaitis, revised edition. Routledge, 2003.

Women World Leaders: Fifteen Great Politicians Tell Their Stories by Laura A. Liswood. Harper San Francisco, 1996.

Web sites

The most important leaders of the twentieth century: www.time.com/time /time100.

Youth Action Net: Connecting Youth to Create Change: www.youthactionnet .org.

LOVE/FRIENDSHIP

A New Look at Love: A Revealing Report on the Most Elusive of All Emotions by Elaine Hatfield and G. William Walster. University Press of America, 2002.

Among Friends: Who We Like, Why We Like Them, and What We Do with Them by Letty Cottin Pogrebin. McGraw-Hill, 1988. Out of print; check your library.

Come Rain or Shine: Friendships Between Women by Linda Bucklin and Mary Keil. Adams Media Corporation, 1999.

The Girlfriends' Bible by Cathy Hamilton. Andrews McMeel Publishing, 2004.

I Know What You Mean: The Power of Friendship in Women's Lives by Ellen Goodman and Patricia O'Brien. Fireside/Simon & Schuster, 2001.

Especially for Young Readers

The Girls' Book of Friendship: Cool Quotes, True Stories, Secrets and More, edited by Catherine Dee. Megan Tingley/Little, Brown, 2001. Ages 10 and up.

The Girls' Book of Love: Cool Quotes, Super Stories, Awesome Advice, and More, edited by Catherine Dee. Megan Tingley/Little, Brown, 2002.

Joys of Friendship: A Celebration of Girlfriends. Hallmark, 2004.

The Simple Truth About Love by Bradley Trevor Greive. Andrews McMeel Publishing, 2005.

MEDICINE AND SCIENCE

Grand Obsession: Madame Curie and Her World by Rosalynd Pflaum. Doubleday, 1989.

Nobel Prize Women in Science: Their Lives, Their Struggles and Momentous Discoveries by Sharon Bertsch McGrayne. National Academies Press, 2001.

Rosalind Franklin: The Dark Lady of DNA by Brenda Maddox. Harper Perennial, 2003. She was on the team of scientists who determined the structure of DNA.

Especially for Young Readers

Black Stars: African American Women Scientists and Inventors by Otha Richard Sullivan, edited by Jim Haskins. Jossey-Bass, 2001. Ages 12 and up.

Celebrating Women in Mathematics and Science, edited by Miriam P. Cooney. National Council of Teachers of Mathematics, 1996. Ages 12 to 15.

Exploring Our Solar System by Sally Ride and Tam O'Shaughnessy. Crown Books for Young Readers, 2003.

Extraordinary Women Scientists by Darlene Stille. Children's Press, 1995. Ages 10 to 13.

Fabulous Female Physicians by Sharon Kirsh. Orca Book Publishers, 2002. Ages 9 to 12.

Sally Ride: Shooting for the Stars by Jane Hurwitz and Sue Hurwitz. Ballantine Books, 1989.

The Sky's the Limit: Stories of Discovery by Women and Girls by Catherine Thimmesh. Houghton Mifflin, 2002. Ages 9 to 12.

To Space and Back: U.S. Astronaut Sally Ride Shares the Adventure of Outer Space by Sally Ride with Susan Okie. HarperCollins, 1986. Ages 6 and up.

Super Women in Science by Kelli Di Domenico. Second Story Press, 2003. Ages 9 to 12.

Studio 2B Focus: Makin' Waves. A Girl Scouts of the U.S.A. book for girls interested in marine biology careers. Available at www.studio2b.org/boutique/.

Young Women of Achievement: A Resource for Girls in Science, Math, and Technology by Frances A. Karnes and Kristin R. Stephens. Prometheus Books, 2002.

Web sites

Girl Start—empowering girls to excel in math, science, and technology: www.girlstart.org.

Sally Ride Science—empowering girls to explore the world of science from astrobiology to zoology and everything in between: www.sallyridescience.com.

Try Science; IBM and more than 4,000 science and technology businesses collaborated to launch this site: www.TryScience.org.

Women in Science: www.astr.ua.edu/4000WS/4000WS.html.

Women of NASA—a project to encourage young women to pursue careers in math, science, and technology: http://questarc.nasa.gov/women/.

ROSA PARKS

Especially for Young Readers

I Am Rosa Parks by Rosa Parks with Jim Haskins. Puffin, 1999. Ages 4 to 8.
Rosa Parks: My Story by Rosa Parks with Jim Haskins. Puffin, 1999. Ages 10 and up.

QUEENS

Catherine de Medici: Renaissance Queen of France by Leona Frieda. Harper Perennial, 2006.
Great Catherine: The Life of Catherine the Great, Empress of Russia by Carolly Erickson. St. Martin's Griffin, 1995. For young adult readers and up.
Isabel of Spain: Catholic Queen by Warren H. Carroll. Christendom Press, 2004.
Queen Victoria: A Personal History by Christopher Hibbert. Da Capo Press, 2001.

Especially for Younger Readers

Behind the Mask: The Life of Queen Elizabeth I by Jane Resh Thomas. Clarion Books, 1998. Ages 10 and up.
Isabel: Jewel of Castilla, Spain, 1466 (The Royal Diaries) by Carolyn Meyer. Scholastic, 2000. Ages 8 to 12.
Victoria: May Blossom of Brittania, England, 1829 (The Royal Diaries) by Anna Kirwan. Scholastic, 2001. Ages 9 to 12.

REFORM/REFORMERS

Jane Addams

Jane Addams: A Biography by James Weber Linn. University of Illinois Press, 2000.
The Jane Addams Reader by Jane Addams, edited by Jean Bethke Elshtain. Basic Books, 2001.

Especially for Younger Readers

Jane Addams: Pioneer Social Worker by Charnan Simon. Children's Press, 1998. Ages 4 and up.

Ela Bhatt

Especially for Younger Readers

Ela Bhatt: Uniting Women in India by Jyotsna Sreenivasan. The Feminist Press at CUNY, 2000. Ages 10 and up.

Máiread Corrigan and Betty Williams

Especially for Younger Readers

Máiread Corrigan & Betty Williams: Making Peace in Northern Ireland by Sarah Buscher and Bettina Ling. The Feminist Press at CUNY, 1998. Ages 9 to 12.

Dorothea Dix

Especially for Younger Readers

Dorothea Dix: Advocate for Mental Health Care by Margaret Muckenhoupt. Oxford University Press, 2004.

The Grimke Sisters

The Grimke Sisters from South Carolina: Pioneers for Women's Rights and Abolition by Gerda Lerner. The University of North Carolina Press, 2006.

Especially for Younger Readers

Sisters Against Slavery: A Story About Sarah and Angelina Grimke by Stephanie Sammartino McPherson. Carolrhoda Books, 2004. Ages 9 to 12.

Mother Jones

Especially for Younger Readers

Mother Jones: Fierce Fighter for Workers' Rights by Judith Pinkerton Josephson. Lerner Publications, 1996. Ages 11 and up.

Florence Kelley

Especially for Younger Readers

Florence Kelley by Carol Saller. Carolrhoda Books, 1997.

Aung San Suu Kyi

Especially for Younger Readers

Aung San Suu Kyi: Standing Up for Democracy in Burma by Bettina Ling. The Feminist Press at CUNY, 1998. Ages 9 to 12.

Rigoberta Menchú

Especially for Younger Readers

Rigoberta Menchú: Defending Human Rights in Guatemala by Michael Silverstone. The Feminist Press at CUNY, 2000. Ages 9 to 12.

Mamphela Ramphele

Especially for Younger Readers

Mamphela Ramphele: Challenging Apartheid in South Africa by Judith Harlen. The Feminist Press at CUNY, 2000. Ages 9 to 12.

Marina Silva

Especially for Younger Readers

Marina Silva: Defending Rainforest Communities in Brazil by Ziporah Hildebrandt. The Feminist Press at CUNY, 2001. Ages 9 to 12.

Web site

The Third Wave Foundation—an organization that builds social justice movements led by young women between the ages of fifteen and thirty: www.thirdwave foundation.org.

SPORTS/ATHLETES

Girl Power: Women on Winning by Carmine DeSena and Jennifer DeSena. Andrews McMeel Publishing, 2002.

The Girls of Summer: The U.S. Women's Soccer Team and How It Changed the World by Jere Longman. Harper Paperbacks, 2001.

Go for the Goal: A Champion's Guide to Winning in Soccer and Life by Mia Hamm. Harper Paperbacks, 2000.

Swimming to Antarctica: Tales of a Long-Distance Swimmer by Lynne Cox. Harvest Books, 2005.

Especially for Younger Readers

Amazing Women Athletes by Jill Bryant. Orca Book Publishers, 2002. Ages 9 to 13.

Let Me Play: The Story of Title IX, the Law That Changed the Future of Girls in America by Karen Blumenthal. Atheneum, 2005. Ages 12 and up.

TECHNOLOGY/COMPUTER SCIENCE/MATH

Careers in Computers (third edition) by Lila B. Stair and Leslie Stair. McGraw-Hill, 2002.

Grace Hopper: Admiral of the Cyber Sea by Kathleen Broome Williams. Naval Institute Press, 2004.

Managing Martians: The Extraordinary Story of a Woman's Lifelong Quest to Get to Mars—and of the Team Behind the Space Robot That Has Captured the Imagination of the World by Donna Shirley. Broadway Books, 1999.

Mothers and Daughters of Invention: Notes for a Revised History of Technology by Autumn Stanley. Rutgers University Press, 1995.

Unlocking the Clubhouse: Women in Computing by Jane Margolis and Allan Fisher. The MIT Press, 2003.

Especially for Younger Readers

Celebrating Women in Mathematics and Science, edited by Miriam P. Cooney. National Counsel of Teachers of Mathematics, 1996. Ages 11 and up.

Cool Careers for Girls in Computers by Ceel Pasternak and Linda Thornburg. Impact Publications, 1999. Ages 10 and up.

Grace Hopper: Computer Whiz by Patricia J. Murphy. Enslow Elementary, 2004. Ages 7 to 9.

Grace Hopper: The First Woman to Program the First Computer in the United States by Christy Marx. Rosen Publishing Group, 2003. Ages 5 and up.

Young Women of Achievement: A Resource for Girls in Science, Math, and Technology by Frances A. Karnes and Kristen R. Stephens. Prometheus Books, 2002.

Web sites

The ADA Project (named for Ada Lovelace)—Internet resources for women in computer science: http://women.cs.cmu.edu/ada/.

African American men and women who have contributed to the advancement of science and engineering: http://webfiles.uci.edu/mcbrown/display/faces.html.

Computer Girl—a bridge from high school to the computer world. www.computergirl.us.

Empowering girls in mathematics, science, and technology: www.girlstart.com.

Engineer Girl! www.engineergirl.org.

Helping students, teachers, and parents plan for careers in technology, engineering, manufacturing, and science: www.gettech.org.

Women in Engineering Organization: www.wieo.org.

Women in mathematics: www.agnesscott.edu/lriddle/women/Women.htm.

Women of NASA—a project to encourage young women to pursue careers in math, science, and technology: http://quest.arc.nasa.gov/women/.

WOW/EM—women on the Web/electronic media: http://eamusic.dartmouth .edu/~wowem/.

HARRIET TUBMAN

Harriet Tubman: The Road to Freedom by Catherine Clinton. Little, Brown, 2004.

Especially for Younger Readers

Wanted Dead or Alive: The True Story of Harriet Tubman by Ann McGovern. Scholastic Paperbacks, 1991. Ages 4 to 8.

OPRAH WINFREY

The Gospel According to Oprah by Marcia Z. Nelson. Westminster John Knox Press, 2005.

Especially for Younger Readers

Oprah Winfrey: I Don't Believe in Failure by Robin Westen. Enslow Publishers, 2005. Ages 9 to 12.

WOMEN IN BUSINESS

The Big Sister's Guide to the World of Work: The Inside Rules Every Girl Must Know by Marcelle Langan DiFalco and Jocelyn Greenky Herz. Fireside/Simon & Schuster, 2004.

Business as Usual: My Entrepreneurial Journey, Profits with Principles by Anita Roddick (founder of The Body Shop). Anita Roddick Press, 2005.

The Difference "Difference" Makes: Women in Leadership, edited by Deborah L. Rhode. Stanford University Press, 2003.

Dream Doll: The Ruth Handler Story by Ruth Handler (creator of the Barbie doll and cofounder of Mattel) with Jacqueline Shannon. Longmeadow Press, 1994. Out of print; check your library.

The Female Advantage by Sally Helgesen. Currency, 1995.

Going to the Top: A Road Map for Success from America's Leading Women Executives by Carol A. Gallagher, Ph.D. with Susan K. Golant. Penguin, 2001.

Hip Girl's Handbook for the Working World by Jennifer Musselman with Patty Fletcher. Wildcat Canyon Press, 2005.

How Jane Won: 55 Successful Women Share How They Grew Up from Ordinary Girls to Extraordinary Women by Sylvia Rimm. Crown Books, 2001.

The Martha Rules: 10 Essentials for Achieving Success as You Start, Grow, or Manage a Business by Martha Stewart. Rodale Books, 2005.

Women at Work by Dayle M. Smith. Prentice Hall, 1999.

Especially for Younger Readers

Business & Industry: Female Firsts in Their Fields by Norma Jean Lutz. Chelsea House Publications, 1999. Ages 10 to 13.

Entrepreneurs by Krista McLuskey. Crabtree Publishing Company, 1999. Ages 9 to 12.

Estée Lauder: Beauty Business Success by Rachel Epstein. Franklin Watts, 2000. Ages 9 to 12.

Girls and Young Women Entrepreneurs: True Stories About Starting and Running a Business, Plus How You Can Do It Yourself by Frances A. Karnes, Ph.D. and Suzanne M. Bean, Ph.D. Free Spirit Publishing, 1997. Ages 11 and up.

Girl Boss: Running the Show Like the Big Chicks, Entrepreneurial Skills and Encouragement for Modern Girls by Stacy Kravetz. Girl Press, 1999.

Madam C. J. Walker by A'lelia Perry Bunders (her great-great granddaughter). Chelsea House Publications, 1991.

Martha Stewart: Successful Businesswoman by Virginia Meachum. Enslow Publishers, 1998.

See Jane Win for Girls: A Smart Girl's Guide to Success by Sylvia Rimm. Free Spirit Publishing, 2003. Ages 10 and up.

Studio 2B Focus: Mind Your Own Business. A Girl Scouts of the U.S.A. book for budding entrepreneurs. Available at www.studio2b.org/boutique/.

Web sites

Explore Career Pathways: www.womenswork.org/girls/.

WRITERS/WRITING

Especially for Younger Readers

African American Women Writers by Brenda Wilkinson. Jossey-Bass, 1999.

Studio B Focus: Write Now. A Girl Scouts of the U.S.A. book for girls who want to be authors. Available at www.studio2b.org/boutique/.

J. K. Rowling by Ann Gaines. Mitchell Lane Publishers, 2004. Ages 9 to 12.

Web sites

Jane Austen: www.austen.com.